# The Physics of the Void

*Exploring the true nature of space*

## Douglas Gibson

# CONTENTS

# ACKNOWLEDGMENTS

Thanks to Nelson Wilby, Andrew Johnson, Richard D Hall, Rupert Sheldrake, Terry Boardman and Ruby for their patience and inspiration.

# INTRODUCTION

This book is an attempt to explore the apparent philosophical gulf between science and spirituality. The scientific and spiritual worldviews appear to be polar opposites, with consciousness itself occupying the ill-defined middle ground. When consciousness itself is treated objectively, however, the best of science and spirituality begin to form one seamless tapestry. But that tapestry can only be constructed when science and spirituality have been unpicked, one thread at a time, and all false assumptions and dogma have been discarded. Some of the axioms of modern science fare surprisingly badly in this process. H P Blavatsky, Rudolf Steiner and many others have contributed to the painstaking process of rationalising spiritual knowledge, but some pieces of the philosophical puzzle still seem to be missing.

Although our consciousness self-evidently exists, the problem revolves around our numinous ideas about what consciousness actually *is*. For conscious experience to be consistent from one person to the next, as seems to be the case, it is here contended that consciousness can only be a manifestation of *number*. This is not a new idea, but can be traced back to Plato and Pythagoras. What is new in this book is the proposition that those numbers must exist within a larger framework - *matrices* or possibly *magic squares* – a model that escapes the strictures of determinism so conscious free will can develop in a causal universe.

This is not strictly a new idea either – it can be found in the grimoires of the medieval alchemists – but is represented here within the context of the Cabala and also within quantum physics.

The wider spiritual reasons for the existence of this gulf in understanding cannot be explored in this small book, but the motives and opportunities for the deliberate misdirection of modern science are considered, starting with a very detailed look at the evidence from the Apollo missions, as these missions played a central role in reinforcing our assumptions about space and matter, assumptions that still underpin much of modern astronomy and physics.

Long-term benevolent and malevolent influences on human development are central to all traditional spiritual worldviews, but are anathema to modern science, which believes that consciousness is an illusory sideshow in a material universe. Consequently, any reassessment of the Apollo missions is dismissed as conspiracy theory, as there can be no conceivable motive for multi-generational deception on such a scale. Modern science is a paradigm that we are constructing from the inside. We are in danger of becoming trapped within that paradigm.

Ideas about magic squares and matrices are entirely the author's and cannot be taken to represent Rudolf Steiner or Anthroposophy.

"The devil's most beautiful ruse is to persuade you that he doesn't exist." – Baudelaire.

# APOLLO

"Hey. We missed the whole thing" - Buzz Aldrin to Neil Armstrong on first seeing the Apollo 11 footage[1]

On January 22nd 1967, Gus Grissom picked a lemon from his garden and hung it on the Apollo 1 capsule to show his frustration at the lamentable state of the Apollo programme. Five days later, Grissom was immolated in that same capsule along with his co-pilots Ed White and Roger Chaffee. All three were doomed as soon as they entered the capsule. The escape hatch could only be opened from the outside, and the pressurised pure oxygen atmosphere inside the capsule was volatile enough to cause aluminium to burn.

NASA management have always maintained that this terrible accident could not have been foreseen, but Ralph Rene and Jarrah White have shown that NASA were already well aware of similar accidents with pressurised oxygen[2]. Thomas Baron's 500 page report into the accident disappeared when Baron, his wife and his step-daughter all died, only days after he completed the report. Baron and his family were found in a car at a railroad crossing but no autopsies were performed. These were not the first or the last convenient deaths in the Apollo era.

Should we entertain the possibility that someone at NASA wanted Grissom out of the way? He had certainly expressed his doubts about the Apollo programme to the press on several occasions, but, as a mechanical engineer and experienced Mercury astronaut, he understood all the technical obstacles that NASA needed to overcome to have any chance of making it to the moon. NASA would have been shooting themselves in the foot by getting rid of Grissom, wouldn't they?

To answer that question, we need to know how much NASA already knew about the feasibility of interplanetary travel. If NASA management were already aware that those technical difficulties were likely to prove insurmountable, then it would have been in their interest to replace Grissom, White and Chaffee with some more malleable characters who understood the paramount importance of projecting the right image in the new television age. Grissom was well aware that holding NASA to account was a dangerous business. He told his wife Betty, *"If there ever is a serious accident in the space program, it's likely to be me.[3]"* According to Ralph Rene, he had already survived two accidents that were not his fault. If NASA were really acting in the public interest, would they have wanted Grissom out of the way?

Did Grissom's death have the effect of making the other astronauts fall into line, and was this unquestioning compliance actually "The right stuff" that NASA needed from the astronauts? In a speech at the Whitehouse on the 25th anniversary of the Apollo 11 landing, Neil Armstrong said: *"The only bird that can talk is the parrot, and he didn't fly very well."* As he said these words, Armstrong appeared to be struggling to control himself. Was he holding back the tears as the press assumed, or wrestling with the possible consequences of saying too much?

According to Steven Greer, Armstrong had been told that he, his wife and family would all be killed if he revealed what really happened during the moon landings[4]. Greer then *assumed* this meant Armstrong had seen UFOs on the moon. Would anyone really have threatened to kill Armstrong just to prevent him from talking about UFOs? Buzz Aldrin claimed to have seen UFOs and wasn't killed. Was Armstrong's life really on the line, and if so, why?

Later in the same speech, Armstrong encouraged the new generation to remove one of *"Truth's protective layers"*. This isn't the usual language of space exploration. Does the truth need protecting, and, if so, who are the custodians protecting, or more likely exploiting the truth, and why? NASA's duty, like any public scientific body, is to discover and reveal the truth, not to keep it from us. Did Armstrong believe that the truth is the preserve of the privileged few who are "worthy", and that it must be kept from us lesser mortals? What is the truth about space exploration, and is there a self-appointed club keeping the truth from us?

The possible sighting of extra-terrestrial life on the Moon or anywhere else is, of course, a fascinating subject that has exercised minds since Giordano Bruno first contemplated the implications of heliocentrism 400 years ago. The answers are beyond the scope of this book, but suffice to say, it's a subject which lends itself easily to flights of fantasy, and NASA management have become very adept at firing and exploiting our imaginations. As Steven Greer has inadvertently shown, the whole subject of UFOs has become a very convenient distraction for NASA. Whenever they are accused of hiding anything, another UFO rumour starts, and the internet echoes to the sound of satisfied emails saying "Ahh, so *that's* what they're hiding".

The rumours that NASA were hiding something started before the Apollo moon shots. Ralph Rene noticed that the photo of Michael Collins' alleged Gemini 10 spacewalk in 1966 was actually just a doctored version of a photo taken inside a zero-G "vomit comet" plane[5]. In the original photo, Collins is surrounded by the internal padding of the zero-G plane, not the blackness of space. In his book; *Ain't Nobody's Business If You Do*, Peter McWilliams says that "Russia's first space walk was later proven to be shot in a studio". The temptation for the Russians and Americans to tell a few fibs in the space race seems to have been irresistible, but, of course, once you start lying, you have to tell more lies to sustain the illusion. Were the Russians and Americans just exaggerating their achievements to win the propaganda war, or were the technical difficulties worse than either side anticipated? If the Americans were already aware that the Russians were at least partially faking it, then Russian silence would have been assured when Kennedy set his sights on the Moon.

Nearly fifty years after the Apollo moon shots, opinion is still divided about what was actually achieved. Perhaps the space race got a little out of hand. Perhaps solar radiation did fog all the photographic film, and we were sold some pre-prepared photos from Stanley Kubrick's studio. Perhaps the big defence contractors realised they could make a few billion from the desperate U.S. government by faking it. Should we care anymore? Haven't we moved on to bigger and better things?

It is the thesis of this book that we most definitely should care. There may be a much deeper and more disturbing motive for faking the moon landings; to prevent us from re-examining our assumptions about space itself, a motive that calls into question some of the fundamentals of modern physics. The Apollo missions created the impression that we can travel indefinitely through space without ill-effect, when this may not actually be the case. Leaving aside the Van Allen radiation belts for the moment, we need to reopen the scientific argument about space itself, or the ether as it used to be known. Einstein himself vacillated on this question his whole life but his General and Special Relativity did not directly address the question. If space has independent existence, just as our everyday experience implies, then what actually *is* space?

Relativity is a multi-dimensional mathematical model of spacetime. It describes the curvature of space, but still does not tell us what space *is*, or whether it has independent existence. Is it simply the nothingness within which everything else exists? Mathematical models are extremely useful, but creating an accurate mathematical model for the slope of a curved roof tells us nothing about the materials from which the roof is built. In this sense, the widespread acceptance of relativity marked a serious departure for modern physics. Since Einstein proposed his model of spacetime, there has been a growing tendency amongst physicists to assume that mathematical models *are* reality, rather than models *of* reality. Just because a mathematical model closely fits the observations still does not mean it *is* reality. This may seem like splitting hairs, but this has profound implications for our understanding of space, and the search for a mythical mathematical "unified theory of everything."

The argument over the existence of the ether was supposedly settled in 1887 when Michelson and Morley's rotating interferometer experiment measured the ether drift at only about one sixth of the expected value. They had expected the Earth to be passing through the ether, or space, at roughly 30 Km/s as it orbits the sun. This lower speed was immediately dismissed by the physics establishment as a "null" result, or experimental error, paving the way for Einstein's abstract conception of space, but Michelson and Morley's experiment was repeated much more carefully, with more sensitive interferometers over a 20 year period by Dayton Miller, and he consistently found an ether drift of around 10 Km/s at the top of Mount Wilson[6]. Miller argued that this was lower than the theoretical value of 30 Km/s because the ether slowed as it passed through the Earth. This would explain why Michelson and Morley had obtained such a low value in their experiment – their interferometer was in a basement. This also suggests that the Earth does not pass entirely freely through space, or the ether, which has implications for Newton's first law: the conservation of momentum.

Einstein and Miller were contemporaries, and Einstein was well aware of the implications of Miller's work. In a letter in July 1925, Einstein said;

*"My opinion about Miller's experiments is the following . . .Should the positive result be confirmed, then the special theory of relativity, and with it the general theory of relativity, in its current form would be invalid. Experimentum summus judex. Only the equivalence of inertia and gravitation would remain, however, they would have to lead to a significantly different theory."* [7]

As president of the American Physical Society, chairman of Physical Sciences at the National Research Council, and member of the National Academy of Sciences, Miller could not be ignored in his own lifetime. After Miller's death, however, his own assistant Robert Shankland set about undermining Miller's results by suggesting that uneven heat distribution around the interferometer had been the cause of Miller's results, when in reality, Miller had actually taken great pains to prevent just such thermal effects[8]. Other experimenters, such as Georges Sagnac, also proved the existence of the ether.

In 2004, the German GOM-Project attempted to redress the institutional pro-relativistic bias by collecting together some 3,789 papers and articles, all critical of Special Relativity that have been published since 1908. Why this deeply unscientific pro-Relativistic bias should exist within academia is another interesting question, but questioning Relativity is certainly still a sackable offence within academia, as Australian mathematician Steve Crothers recently found to his cost.

Relativity is really a 4-dimensional mathematical model incorporating Newton's Laws, and calculating velocities and fuel requirements for interplanetary travel still rests almost entirely on Newton's theory of universal gravitation, but, if we ignore NASA's self-serving evidence, Newton's "universal" theory has only been tested within a few hundred miles of the Earth. This begs the question: Why was Newton's theory of universal gravitation enshrined as "law" when it can never be proven to be universal? If Newton's inverse-square gravity was the only force holding the solar system together, we should have spiralled into the sun a long time ago. Croatian physicist Roger Boscovich modified Newton's gravitational model in the 18th century with a force curve that included attraction *and* repulsion — a much more stable model than Newton's, though even this model still didn't take space itself, *the ether* into account.

# THE ROCKETS

Why is the scientific establishment so keen to embrace Newton, Einstein and latterly Hawking, but so quick to dismiss Boscovich, Miller and Tesla? If the ether exists, it may not be possible to climb aboard a rocket and fly to the moon, however large the rocket. Wernher von Braun, writing in *The Conquest of the Moon* in the early '50s, said that, for a round trip to the moon, the rockets would have to be; *"Taller than New York's Empire State Building, and weigh about 10 times the tonnage of the Queen Mary, or some 800,000 tons."*

A few years later, Von Braun designed the comparatively miniscule 3,000 ton Saturn 5 rockets, which allegedly did the same job despite being only 0.38% of the mass of his original calculations. There were some improvements in rocket propulsion in the intervening decade, but was there really a 250-fold improvement in rocket efficiency? At some point, Von Braun seems to have traded the dream of space travel for a fantasy. Dream and fantasy were always closely connected in Von Braun's life. His mentor in Germany, Hermann Oberth was technical adviser for Fritz Lang's 1929 sci-fi film *Frau Im Mond* (Woman in the Moon). Wikipedia says of this film:

"Several prescient technical /operational features are presented during the film's 1920s launch sequence, which subsequently came into common operational use during America's postwar space race." Von Braun also worked closely with Walt Disney in the 1950s.

Bill Kaysing was the first person to publically decry the Apollo landings. He had actually worked at Rocketdyne, the manufacturers of the Saturn 5 engines for 7 years. Though not an engineer by training, he had seen enough to know that no one was going to the moon on a Saturn 5 rocket. Rocketdyne's F1 engines were theoretically powerful enough to propel the fully-laden Saturn 5, but were notoriously unreliable. Kaysing's colleague Bill Wood knew that the reliable but less powerful B1 engine could easily be made to look like the F1 engine. To have produced seven safe but spectacular Apollo lift-offs in succession, NASA must have used the modified B1 engines, but that would mean the rockets that we saw lifting off from Cape Canaveral could only have carried enough fuel to reach low Earth orbit.

Bill Wood has a BSc in Aerospace Engineering, a MSc in Mechanical Engineering, has worked on US Air Force rockets and ICBMs, on the Delta Satellite launch vehicle, and he chaired the ASME propulsion technical committee. What Bill Wood doesn't know about rocket propulsion is not worth knowing. David S. Percy interviewed him for his *Dark Moon* book, published in 1999:

*"Film footage of the Saturn V launch records the five F-1 motors producing an 800 foot long highly fuel-rich exhaust plume together with extensive atmospheric after-burn," Bill Wood says. "These exhaust plumes are dark for the first eight feet from the end of the nozzle, then ignition of a very fuel-rich exhaust occurs in the atmosphere. The recorded effect is not typical of other known rocket engines utilising the same propellants. So could it be that the rocket motors in this Saturn V were in fact the smaller B-1 engines, inserted into the centre of an F-1 motor shell?" Bill asks. "These B-1 engines were proven rocket motors with lower thrust, originally used in the Saturn 1B rocket." He continued: "These substitutes would then have had extra kerosene injected into the annular space between the rocket motors. This fuel would then be vaporised and burned in the atmosphere. While it would not provide*

*much increase in thrust, it would have been reliable, and would also account for the 'flame-thrower' effect visible at launch." "Why would this be done," we asked? "The reason would have been to make the rocket appear to be more powerful than it really was – and we all know that flame-throwers produce very little thrust!"* [9]

In 1996, Kaysing tried to sue Jim Lovell, the Apollo 13 commander for libel. Bill Wood was due to testify to support Kaysing's case, but had a massive stroke before the case came to court, so another highly-qualified Apollo critic was denied a platform.

If we ignore the terrifying spectre of an epic conspiracy to defraud the public and distort the scientific understanding of space for the moment, what evidence do we have that the Apollo astronauts actually made it to the moon?

We all saw the Apollo astronauts climb aboard the Saturn V rockets and launch into the blue yonder in front of cheering crowds, so we know they at least made it to Low Earth Orbit. Some have suggested there was an opportunity to deceive us even at this early stage. Some of the launch pads at Cape Canaveral had blast rooms (rubber rooms) 40 feet below ground, that the astronauts could reach via an escape chute in an emergency. James Burke was given access to one of these blast rooms for the BBC. The astronauts would, however, have had to use the lift to descend the 300 ft from the top of the rocket to the chute entrance, so we can probably discount the idea that any of the astronauts remained on Earth.

# THE PHOTOS

Once the rockets had climbed out of sight, we were completely dependent on images supplied by NASA. The debate over those images is as heated as ever and would fill several volumes on their own, although the Apollo defenders have found themselves increasingly on the defensive. Leaving aside arguments about multiple light sources and backscattering, the clarity of the lunar photos has become an issue in itself. The Haselblad cameras were fixed to the front of the astronauts' suits, and they had to wear heavy gloves, so they could not focus or frame any of the photos, and yet the vast majority are perfectly focussed and framed. If they were faked, they must have been taken by a professional photographer – old habits die hard!

Jay Weidner has also noticed that there is a clear dividing line between foreground and background in all the wider shots, suggesting they were taken in a large studio[10]. In many of the photos, the foreground and background are both in focus – apparently an infinite depth of focus, which is only possible with a tripod and a pinhole camera, neither of which were available to the astronauts on the moon.

During the Apollo 16 mission in 1972, Charlie Duke placed a cellophane-covered photo of his family on the moon and recorded it for posterity. But Andrew Johnson has pointed out that, far from lying flat, the photo should have curled up very quickly in the $100^0$C daytime temperatures[11].

How the astronauts' suits were able to dissipate this searing heat has also never been satisfactorily explained by NASA. We'll have to give NASA the benefit of the doubt on the perennial issue of the visibility of stars, as the high light levels in the sunlit areas may have made the stars invisible.

All arguments about the minutiae of the photos have become a side-show, however, since Ukrainian photo analyst Oleg Oleynik published his high resolution digital parallax analysis of the Apollo 15 photos on the Aulis.com website[12]. His paper, titled *"A stereoscopic method of verifying Apollo lunar surface images"* proves conclusively that ALL of the hills, valleys and craters in the Apollo 15 photos were actually within 300 meters of the camera. According to the official Apollo records and maps, however, Mount Hadley was 30 Km away, St George's crater 5 Km away, and Rima Hadley bow was 7 Km away from the camera. Either the Apollo 15 photos were faked in a very large studio, or the moon is actually in Lilliput!

Oleynik's analysis is so accurate, he was able to prove that at least 3 different techniques were used to create the illusion of distance and perspective in the photos. A scale replica of Mount Hadley, tens of meters high rather than thousands, was used in some of the photos, so that small movements of the camera produced relatively large changes in perspective. Good old-fashioned cut and paste was used in the foreground of some shots, creating impossible distortions when stereoscopically compared, but, most interesting of all, large background screens leaning in towards the camera were used to create realistic changes of perspective in the background. Someone with very deep pockets went to enormous lengths to make the photos as realistic as possible, but they simply do not stand up in the high definition digital age. The moving stereoscopic gifs in Oleynik's online article tell the whole story.

For the clearest results, the large suspended screens would have needed to be highly reflective. Stanley Kubrick perfected front screen projection onto giant reflective Scotchlite screens on the set of *2001, A*

*Space Odyssey*, so he was certainly the man for the job. Carl James has documented Kubrick's connections to NASA in his lecture series called *The Kubrick Conundrum*. Kubrick appears to have left a string of clues to this effect in his later films. Anyone wanting to know how a successful film director could become entangled in such an appalling deception need only watch Kubrick's final film, the appropriately titled; *Eyes Wide Shut*. This disturbing film may also be one of the few clues we have as to the motives for a deception of this scale. Only those who enjoy manipulating and exploiting the whole of humanity would go to such extreme lengths to hide the truth. The individuals controlling this game embody the absolute antithesis of Christian selflessness . . .

So the Apollo 15 photos at least are fake. Oleynik's study should have been headline news. Instead, scientists continue to focus on their increasingly compartmentalised subjects and assume that the bigger questions will be answered by some abstract mathematical unified theory of everything, and the media are frightened of challenging the scientific consensus, so the charade continues. Was it Hitler who said; *"The bigger the lie, the more it will be believed."?* Perhaps, as you read this, someone is being tasked with creating a plausible explanation why the Apollo 15 photos had to be faked, as a damage limitation exercise in case Oleynik's work attracts too much attention. Or perhaps they don't feel they will need to, as they know the mainstream media are nervous of anything that is such an affront to the status quo, even if it's true! As no prominent scientists dared to publically challenge NASA about the moon landings at the time, mainstream physicists and astronomers have found it politic to keep their doubts to themselves ever since.

*"It's easier to fool people than to convince them that they have been fooled."* – Mark Twain.[13]

# THE MOONROCKS

Hard evidence doesn't come any harder than the moon rocks - According to Wikipedia;

*"Of the 270 Apollo 11 moon rocks and Apollo 17 Goodwill Moon Rocks that were given to the nations of the world by the Nixon administration, approximately 180 are currently unaccounted for."* [14] If Tricky Dicky had presented you with a moon rock, would it have taken pride of place on your mantelpiece? The Dutch National Museum was particularly disappointed in 2009 to find that their Apollo 11 moon rock was actually a piece of petrified wood. Given the God-like status enjoyed by NASA, it's a wonder no-one cited this as proof that there are trees on the Moon, followed by a flurry of speculation on the internet about why NASA are hiding the trees on the Moon! That particular moon rock certainly originated on the Earth, and it turns out there are many more genuine moon rocks here, on the Earth.

Starting in the late 1960s, AMLAMP, the Antarctic Meteorite Location And Mapping Project [15] has located over 35,000 meteorites in Antarctica. A small percentage of these are Lunaites; small moon rocks that have been hurled into cislunar space by large meteorite impacts on the Moon, and have fallen to Earth. James Head has calculated that any meteorite that creates a crater 450 meters or more in diameter on the moon theoretically has the kinetic energy to throw moon rocks back to the Earth[16]. Like all meteorites, lunaites should be present all over the Earth, but are easiest to find in deserts and polar regions where they are not hidden by vegetation. Lunar meteorites from the Sahara and Middle East can even be purchased from meteorite collectors' websites, and yet NASA still insist that their Moonrocks could only have travelled to Earth in their Apollo capsules.

Suspicions abound about the purpose of Von Braun's trip to Antarctica in January 1967. Ostensibly, they were there to test equipment in the freezing Antarctic environment, but this could have been done much more easily and effectively closer to home. Antarctica would certainly have been the best place to look for clean, sterile moon rocks. Moon rocks from more temperate regions would almost certainly be contaminated with lichen and bacteria, giving away their real origin. Critics have pointed out that the total mass of officially recognised lunar meteorites collected over the last 50 years is only a fraction of the 380 Kgs of moon rocks provided by the Apollo astronauts, suggesting that Von Braun would have needed several hundred years to collect such a large mass of them in Antarctica.

Jarrah White[17] has taken on this whole complex argument in his *Moonfaker* video series. In the decades since the Apollo missions, we have been given a string of seemingly plausible reasons why the Apollo moonrocks could only have been brought back by the astronauts. All meteorites that fall to Earth have a thin fusion crust; a surface layer of rock that has been melted by the heat generated as they passed through the Earth's upper atmosphere. The moon rock features that have been cited as indisputable proof that they were brought here from the moon are;

1/    The absence of fusion crust, as they were ostensibly brought here by the astronauts.

2/    The presence of rare isotopes caused by exposure to the solar wind.

3/    The presence of Helium 3.

4/    The ratios of elements within the rocks, particularly rare elements like Titanium.

5/    The very low moisture levels.

6/    The ratio of Ferric to Ferrous iron.

7/    The presence of micrometeorite damage – micrometeorites burn up in the Earth's upper
      Atmosphere, so terrestrial rocks do not have micrometeorite "pits" on their surface.

Jarrah White has pointed out that, with the right equipment, all of these "lunar" features can be replicated here, on Earth. Fusion crust can be removed from a meteorite's surface. Heating rocks in a vacuum chamber for a few days will reduce moisture levels and change ferric/ferrous iron ratios. Firing sand-sized particles through a high velocity gas gun will replicate micrometeorite damage, and bombarding rocks in a particle accelerator will replicate the effects of the solar wind.[18]

Perhaps more interesting though, is White's discovery that Eucrite and Howardite meteorites, which are much more abundant than lunar meteorites, have the same ratio of elements as the Apollo rocks. Eucrites and Howardites are not classified as lunar meteorites, but are so similar that they have often been mistaken for lunar meteorites. This might explain the apparent paucity of lunar meteorites on Earth. The ratio of lunar to Martian meteorites collected on Earth is much lower than theory would predict – is it possible that the bulk of lunar meteorites have been misclassified, and that they are more common here on Earth than NASA would have us believe?

# RADIATION

Sir Bernard Lovell made several trips to Russia in the late 1950s and early '60s, and was given access to Russian space technology. At the time, the Russians appeared to be well ahead in the space race, but Lovell reported that;

*"The Russians could see no effective way of protecting cosmonauts from the lethal effects of solar radiation."* [19]

In 2009, Lovell revealed that he had been exposed to lethal radiation on one of his Russian trips[20]. He believed this was a deliberate attempt to incapacitate him, so he would be unable to use the Jodrell Bank radio telescope to track Russian satellites, but, if they were so far ahead, did they really need to try to kill Lovell? To prevent anyone tracking them, they would have needed to sabotage the telescope rather than target Lovell. Could it be that Lovell had learnt a bit too much about the real level of radiation in space, and was thus a threat to Russian *and* American plans?

In February 1958, the 14Kg American Explorer 1 satellite, equipped with a Geiger counter, was put into an elliptical orbit between 225 and 1,580 miles above the Earth. The Geiger counter readings went off the scale roughly 600 miles above the Earth, and in the March 1959 edition of Scientific American, James Van Allen reported that;

*"We have encountered a very high intensity of radiation which is of the order of 1,000 times as could be attributed to cosmic rays as ordinarily understood."*

This statement, combined with the Russian research, should have been enough to stymie all plans for manned space travel, but instead, the Americans seem to have decided to sweep this inconvenient truth aside. Van Allen himself later recanted and said;

*"The claim that radiation exposure during the Apollo missions would have been fatal to the astronauts is nonsense."* [21] It's not clear what caused this volte-face by Van Allen. Perhaps he was lucky to get the chance to recant. Others who have presented unpalatable truths to NASA have not been so lucky.

Contrary to Van Allen's latter words, the evidence suggests that the radiation problem did not just go away sometime between 1959 and 1969. Writing in *Prospects for Interstellar Travel* in 1992, John H Mauldin said; *"Cosmic particles are dangerous, come from all sides, and require at least 2 meters of solid shielding all around living organisms. Earth's atmosphere provides the equivalent of about 10 meters of shielding."*

Writing in Scientific American in March 2006, Eugene Parker proposed 5 meters of shielding from cosmic rays of only 2 GeV, so 500 tons of water would be needed to protect even a small capsule.

*". . . Engineers could use ethylene ($C_2H_2$) which has the further advantage that it can be polymerised to polyethylene, a solid, thereby avoiding the necessity for a tank to contain it. Even so, the required mass would be at least 400 tons – still not feasible. . . Pure hydrogen would be lighter, but would require a highly pressurised vessel."*

Thin layers of metallic shielding like aluminium cause particle fragmentation, which can actually increase the total amount of radiation within a space vehicle, and as recently as 2008, Reuters ran an article titled: *What's Keeping us from Mars? Space Rays, Say Experts,*[22] which states;

*"Cosmic rays are so dangerous and so poorly understood that people are unlikely to get to Mars or even back to the Moon, until better ways are found to protect astronauts."*

There are two doughnut-shaped Van Allen radiation belts surrounding the Earth. The inner belt extends from around 1,000 Km above the Earth's equator to about 5,000 Km, and the outer extends from about 15,000 to 25,000 Km above the Earth's equator. Particles released from the sun during solar flares are trapped by the Earth's magnetic field and can dramatically increase the levels of radiation within the belts. Particles travelling near light speed will arrive from the sun within 15 minutes or so of a solar flare erupting. The overall level of sunspot activity follows a roughly 11 year cycle, but individual sunspots are completely unpredictable.

All the Mercury, Soyuz, Vostock, Voskhod and early Apollo flights stayed within 1,000 Km of Earth, as did Skylab, MIR, the International Space Station, all shuttle flights and the Hubble telescope. The Russians claim that they sent 2 tortoises and some mealworms and wine flies around the moon and back in 1968 on their Zond 5 mission. If this is true, this means they flew almost a thousand times further than all the preceding flights, with no crew on board to make course corrections along the way! This astonishing claim has been cited as proof that the Van Allen belts are not lethal, but the Russians seem to have selected only the most radiation-tolerant species for this trip, if indeed they really did travel as far as the moon. The lethal dose (LD50) for a tortoise is 15,000 Rads compared to only 400 Rads for a man.

To explain how the Apollo astronauts avoided getting fried before they had even made it through the Van Allen radiation belts surrounding the Earth, Apollo defenders claim that the astronauts were just lucky to miss any major solar flares, but this statement simply does not match the official record. The National Oceanic and Atmospheric

Administration in the U.S. keeps a record of all solar flares. They are classified as major or minor, but even minor ones can deliver a lethal dose of radiation to anyone travelling beyond the Earth's protective atmosphere. Jarrah White checked all the flares during each Apollo mission and found the Apollo astronauts were exposed to anything from 81 flares on Apollo 17 (8 of which were major) to 268 flares on Apollo 15 (1 major) during their missions.[23]

Even using conservative radiation estimates, this is enough radiation to have killed all the astronauts as the thin-skinned Apollo Command module offered little protection. In August 1972, only months after the Apollo 16 mission, a massive solar flare caused power failures across North America. NASA seem to have muddied the waters by claiming that there was a massive flare *during* the Apollo 16 mission,[24] and the fact that the astronauts survived proves that their radiation protection was effective ! A false retrospective circular argument – can't argue with that!

NASA always responds to this evidence with vague platitudes about special spacesuit linings and manoeuvring the Command module to place the bulk of the craft between the sun and the astronauts to shield them. But, as Ralph Rene pointed out, if these magic suits really exist, why aren't they in use at every nuclear power station in the world? Where were they when we needed them at Three Mile Island, Chernobyl and Fukushima? Before anyone claims that solar and cosmic radiation are not comparable to the radiation in nuclear power plants, no, they're not directly comparable – solar and cosmic radiation are *higher energy* and therefore *more dangerous!*

Modern space salesmen like Elon Musk, Robert Zubrin and Dennis Tito either accept NASA's magic spacesuit blandishments or give us vague reassurances about alternative radiation protection provided by powerful electric or magnetic fields. Apart from the possible medical side-effects, such fields require enormous amounts of power and heavy electrical equipment, which means they are just as impracticable as the 3 feet of lead shielding that the Russians proposed 50 years ago. In the meantime, they continue to peddle their CGI space dreams to an impressionable public, thereby putting pressure on politicians to release yet more public money to chase lucrative, unrealistic space fantasies.

# THE MIRACULOUS HEATSHIELD

Radiation is not the only problem that NASA has had to retrospectively airbrush out of the Apollo story. Writing in Nexus magazine in 2015 (*NASA's moon mission technology problems: how did Apollo ever make it to the Moon?*), Phil Kouts pointed out that NASA appear to be starting completely from scratch with their Constellation and Orion programs. Problems which NASA apparently overcame in a matter of months 50 years ago now seem to be insurmountable. The most serious problem is the heatshield. Vessels returning from the Moon enter the Earth's upper atmosphere travelling at over 11 Km/s. Meteorites burn white hot and disintegrate as they enter the Earth's upper atmosphere and the only thing protecting any spacecraft from a similar fate is its heatshield. In a direct re-entry, the heat generated is sufficient to melt anything other than tungsten or diamond. Tungsten is too heavy and 3-meter-wide diamonds are hard to find, so NASA had to look for other ways around the problem.

The Russians claim to have used skip re-entry on their Zond 5 mission. In theory, bouncing the spacecraft off the upper atmosphere slows the spacecraft, and allows the heatshield to cool down for 40-90 minutes before it falls to Earth at reduced speed. This sounds good in theory, but, even if it could be made to work, the asymmetric forces on the spacecraft would cause it to tumble, head over heels at high speed.

When a flat, spinning stone skips across the surface of a lake, it is only the lateral rotation that stabilises the stone and prevents it from flipping over, so allowing it to skip. If it's not spinning, it doesn't work. WW 2 bouncing bombs rotated on a horizontal axis to stabilise them and make them bounce. Even if a small capsule could be made to bounce off the upper atmosphere without centrifuging the astronauts first, such a re-entry would be extremely unpredictable – who can accurately control the bounce of a skipping stone?

The Russians claim that the monostability of their Soyuz craft was the key to their successful re-entry. Monostability simply means keeping the center of gravity very low so that the craft is self-righting in the latter stages of freefall, but this would not prevent tumbling in a skip re-entry. If the Russian mealworms and tortoises really did survive the Zond 5 re-entry, they would have been centrifuged and cooked. Human crew are more vocal in their objection to such maltreatment.

Astonishingly, confusion abounds about what re-entry method was actually used for the Apollo missions. Apollo flight director Chris Kraft has stated that;

*"Because the velocity is so high, if you tried to come in directly, the heat-shield requirements would be too great. So what we did was get them into the atmosphere, skip it out to kill off some of the velocity, and then bring it back in again. That made the total heat pulse on the heat-shield of the spacecraft considerably lower."* [25]

Astronauts Thomas Stafford of Apollo 10 and Al Worden of Apollo 15, however, say it was a direct re-entry. Clearly, somebody is lying. In fact, Al Worden said; *"Chris Kraft is a bad guy. If we could feed him to a bomb we would."* [26] The astronauts would certainly know the difference between skip re-entry and direct re-entry. Direct re-entry would be short (about 8 mins), very hot, and involve high G-forces, whereas skip re-entry is two-stage, with 40-90 minutes of weightless freefall in the middle. Why would the flight director need to change history? Had the original Apollo narrative become "unsustainable" in the light of NASA's failure to reproduce the miraculous Apollo heat-shield that could apparently withstand the heat of direct re-entry?

These flat contradictions have been smoothed over by the ill-defined notion of *double-dip re-entry,* or was it *double-bluff re-entry?* But really, Chris Kraft has already let the cat out of the bag. No one has been able to develop a heat-shield that can cope with the enormous heat generated by re-entering the Earth's atmosphere at 11 Km/s. The December 2014 unmanned Orion test flight travelled only 5,800 Km from the Earth and used ceramic heat-shield tiles similar to the Columbia Shuttle tiles that failed in 2003, costing the lives of all 7 crew. The Orion capsule re-entered at around 8.9 Km/s, generating temperatures of 2,200°C, which is 500°C hotter than any Shuttle re-entry, but still 500°C short of the temperatures the Apollo capsules allegedly withstood.[27]

So where is this Apollo heat-shield material that withstood the higher Apollo re-entry speeds and temperatures and worked every time? The NASA public relations department has had to work overtime on this one. The 2005 Architecture Study for the cancelled Constellation program revealed that; *"The Apollo ablative Thermal Protection System (Avcoat 5061) no longer exists. Qualification of new or replacement materials will require extensive analysis and testing."* [28]

Three years later, a 2008 report by the Government Accountability Office stated:

*"According to the Orion program executive, the Orion Project originally intended to use the heat shield from the Apollo program as a fallback technology for the Orion thermal protection system, but was unable to recreate the Apollo material",* and also that; *"facilities available from the Apollo era for testing large-scale heat shields no longer exist."* [29] In 2009, they were still digging;

*". . . After some difficulties, NASA was successful in recreating the material. Because it uses a framework with many honeycomb-shaped*

*cells, each of which must be individually filled without voids or imperfections, it may be difficult to repeatedly manufacture to consistent standards. According to program officials, during the Apollo program the cells were filled by hand. The contractor plans to automate the process for the Orion Thermal Protection System, but this capability is still being developed."* [30]

So much for technological trickle-down! After trying the old "Oh dear, we lost the recipe" excuse, and realising that wasn't really good enough for a crucial element of the entire Apollo story, they had to find some anonymous technicians to blame. After all, technicians' hands were so much steadier in days of old; able to fill the heatshield honeycomb with no bubbles at all, something which tremulous, modern hands could not possibly accomplish! Even when the NASA magicians' sleight of hand is in plain sight, there appears to be a collective reluctance to question the illusion; to be first to break the spell.

Phil Kouts has shown that all the apparent achievements of the Apollo era seem to have crumbled to dust in the intervening years. NASA are now relying on Russian RD-180 engines in their Atlas rockets, even though they are less powerful than the F-1 engines that the Saturn 5 rockets allegedly used. They say they will be using Elon Musk's Falcon 9 Heavy rockets in future, though they only exist on paper at the moment (2016). They say they can't rebuild the second-stage J2 engines from the Apollo era because, according to the GAO; *"The number of planned changes is such that, according to NASA review boards, the effort essentially represents a new engine development."* [31]

Their magic spacesuits would be invaluable in the nuclear industry, and also in fire-fighting due to their infinite capacity to resist radiation and dissipate heat, but they only seem to be available for low Earth orbit photo-opportunities. They claim to have solved the heat-shield problem all those years ago, but now find it too difficult to *"manufacture to consistent standards."* There are even larger gaps in the Lunar Module technology. Neither descent nor ascent stages worked successfully on Earth. The lower stage had a flat upper surface, which would have made the upper stage extremely unstable when lifting off from the lunar surface. And, of course, they conveniently lost 700 boxes of original Apollo data tapes.

NASA's complete inability to salvage any of the Apollo technology, or even to supply lunar surface radiation data which would be crucial to the success of any future missions, led ultimately to the cancellation of the entire Constellation Program. One of the reasons cited for not returning to the Moon was the difficulty of escaping from lunar gravitation (the lunar "gravity well") after a landing. But the American administration is now talking about a mission to Mars, where gravity is twice as strong. Having decided that returning to the Moon is beyond our current technical capabilities, they've decided to sell us a dream that is twice as implausible.

In order to create any semblance of credibility for future manned space adventures, the rhetorical acrobatics are being stepped up again. Lockheed Martin admitted that there were problems with *"the compression pads . . .which fill in the joints on the heat shield between Orion's Command Module and Service Module. Their purpose is to carry the structural loads generated during launch, space operations, and pyroshock separation (explosive bolts) of the two modules. . .New and more resilient thermal insulating compression pads. . . are needed because the current 2-D pads used on Orion's recently completed maiden test flight. . . are only suitable for Earth orbit return."* [32]

Once again this raises the obvious question of how this identical problem was solved 50 years ago. But never fear - even though they have been unable to recreate the miraculous Apollo heat-shield, those NASA boffins have come up with another brilliant solution; *"An innovative 3-D woven material"* has been developed as *"a direct result of lessons learned from Orion's inaugural mission."* So we can all look forward to the real-life industrial applications of yet another timely NASA innovation. But before we all rush off and invest our life savings in this brilliant (unannounced) breakthrough, we need to ask some questions. Is this "innovative 3-D woven material" being woven by specially-trained hands? And will these hands ever be able to recreate this 3-D woven material outside of NASA's and Lockheed Martin's own special labs? Will any of NASA's brilliant innovations ever transfer successfully from glossy video to the real world?

*"Don't worry. Matt Damon won't get stuck on Mars. NASA can't get him there".* (The Washington Post, revealing more than they intended, 2/10/2015.)

# LASERS

As the advent of the internet has given the public much greater access to documentation and film footage, the holes in the Apollo story have become increasingly obvious. What better way to patch up the holes than by using the latest technology to reassure everyone? After all, technology has advanced enormously since the '60s, and using the latest tech implies that the most successful and innovative minds find nothing implausible in the Apollo story.

For the 2009 BBC Horizon 40th anniversary documentary, Professor Brian Cox was sent to the McDonald Observatory in Texas to witness a powerful laser beam being bounced off the Moon.[33] We are told that small retro-reflectors about 18" square were placed on the Moon by the Apollo 11 and 14 astronauts (and one twice the size by Apollo 15), and that laser light reflected back to the Earth proves that the retro-reflectors are indeed on the surface of the Moon. But this reflected light would be impossible to discern. The reflectivity (albedo) of the surface of the Moon varies between dark and light areas, with an average value of around 0.12 – otherwise, we wouldn't have moonlight.

The LOLA instrument on the Lunar Reconnaissance Orbiter has measured albedo values between 0.03 and 0.14 at 1064nm, with a value of 0.07 for the Sea of Tranquility. That means 7% of the light that hits the Sea of Tranquility is reflected back. Even laser light slowly spreads out on the 238,000 mile journey to the Moon, so any laser fired from Earth will cover a circular area of roughly 6.5 kilometres diameter by the time it reaches the lunar surface. If that area covers one of the retroreflectors, then an area of roughly 0.5m² within that circle will reflect 14 times as much light as it would have done if the retro-reflector was not there. This is a 0.00001% increase in the total reflected laser light.

Even if the retro-reflectors were perfectly made, the reflected light would still diverge on its journey back to Earth. This tiny amount of reflected light would be too small to measure against the background of randomly reflected laser light, bearing in mind that the albedo of every square kilometre of the lunar surface will be slightly different from the next. A large pale area of the lunar surface would reflect more light than a retro-reflector. Are we to believe polychromatic light (sunlight) reflects from the lunar surface, but monochromatic (laser) light does not? We would need to know the albedo of the lunar surface around the retro-reflectors, before and after the Apollo missions, to at least 5 decimal places to be able to say for certain that the reflectors are there.

Even if we discount this argument on the basis that retro-reflected light is coherent and surface-reflection is not, lasers were being bounced off the Moon long before the Apollo missions, so how does bouncing a laser off the Moon prove anything? On 5th November 1963, the New York Times reported ;

*"A concentrated beam of light has been bounced off the Moon and detected on Earth by a Soviet observatory in the Crimea. The feat, reported today by TASS, the Soviet press agency, duplicates an experiment conducted late last year by engineers of the Massachusetts Institute of Technology."* [34]

This was confirmed in a December 1966 National Geographic article titled *The Laser's Bright Magic.* Are we to believe that MIT and the Crimean Astrophysical Observatory were just lucky to find places on the Moon with high enough albedo to bounce a signal back to Earth? One intriguing suggestion is that the Moon was carefully scanned for the most reflective areas *before* the Apollo missions, and that these areas were then chosen as the putative Apollo 11, 14 and 15 landing sites, so that the increased reflectivity could later be attributed to the presence of the retro-reflectors, even if there aren't really any on the Moon! (Apollo 12, 16 and 17 did not take retro-reflectors.)

Lasers were being bounced off the Moon seven years before the Apollo missions, and yet Professor Brian Cox OBE FRS would have us believe that performing the same trick today is proof positive that retro-reflectors were placed there by the Apollo astronauts. On the 46th anniversary of the Apollo 11 landing, Prof. Cox tweeted; "If you don't think Apollo 11 landed on Moon, you are a colossal *** end and should get a new brain." Presumably, he means a brain that is comfortable within a permanent state of cognitive dissonance; a brain that does not have the courage to question scientific orthodoxy.

# THE LUNAR RECONNAISANCE ORBITER

In 1994, the Clementine Orbiter spent two months surveying the lunar surface with high resolution cameras and a LIDAR (Laser Image Detection And Ranging) scanner. This LIDAR sent 10ns pulses from a 1064nm Yttrium-Aluminium-Garnet infrared laser down to the lunar surface, and precisely timed the return signals over 300 orbits to build up a topographical map of the lunar surface to about 40m vertical resolution. This will only work if the laser does indeed bounce off every square kilometre of the lunar surface. The very existence of topographical maps of the Moon proves that return signals can be detected from every part of the Moon, whether there are retro-reflectors there or not. We are told Clementine was rendered inoperable in May '94 when an attitude controller jammed on for 11 minutes, using all the fuel, and putting the orbiter into an 80 rpm spin.

Since 2009 the Lunar Reconnaissance Orbiter has been mapping the lunar surface using another laser altimeter, split into 5 beams and equipped with faster electronics, called the LOLA detector (Lunar Orbiter Laser Altimeter). We are told the data is being used to find mineral resources and safe landing sites for future lunar missions as part of NASA's Lunar Precursor Robotics Program. The eagerly anticipated high resolution LRO camera images of the Apollo landing sites were released in March 2011, but are only 0.5m resolution and have a smooth monochromatic quality, reminiscent of CGI. Nevertheless, they were used to reassure the public once again about the veracity of the Apollo legend. Professor Mark Robinson, chief scientist for the LRO camera said:

*"From the LROC images, it is now certain that the American flags are still standing and casting shadows at all of the sites, except Apollo 11."* [35] Unfortunately this assertion, like so many of NASA's statements, is not really the self-evident proof that it initially appears to be. Here on the Earth's surface, we are protected from solar and cosmic radiation by our atmosphere, but, even in low earth orbit, this radiation can be damaging. Jarrah White noted that a flag hung outside the Russian MIR space station was reduced to threads in less than 12 months.[36]

There is no atmosphere to protect the Apollo flags on the Moon, and yet NASA would have us believe that their flags have survived nearly half a century of exposure to solar and cosmic radiation. Either they are made of the same miraculous material as the space suits, or we have to consider the disturbing possibility that the CGI –like quality of the LRO images may be more than coincidental. They've certainly had enough time to load the original Clementine images into a computer database and use CGI software to embellish them, to create the illusion of higher resolution. At 0.5m resolution, no Earth-bound telescope will ever be in a position to contradict them.

Whilst trying to find out more about the so-called "Face on Mars", Richard Hoagland learned a few things that are even more interesting than any putative Martian archaeology:

"Neither NASA nor Congress had anything to say about where Michael Malin had pointed his Mars Orbiter camera. In an unprecedented move, NASA had decided to sell the rights to all of the data collected by the Observer to Malin himself, in an exclusive arrangement that gave Malin godlike powers over when, or even if, he decided to release any data the camera collected. This private contractor arrangement not only neatly absolved NASA from any responsibility as to what was photographed with an instrument and mission paid for by the taxpayers of the United States, but it gave Malin the right to embargo data for up to half a year, if he so chose. . . . Malin even moved his entire private company, Malin Space Science Systems (which held the actual Mars Observer camera contract) away from ASU in Arizona and JPL in California to San Diego. . . Curiously, however, the move did put him right across the street from one of the world's largest "supercomputer" facilities. . . where he could literally hand-carry digital imaging tapes back and forth. . ." [37]

In 2007, Google announced its $30 million Lunar X-Prize for the first privately funded team to land a robot on the Moon, travel 500m and send high resolution images back to Earth, with a bonus prize for "capturing images of the remains of Apollo programme hardware". The time limit to claim the prize was the end of 2017. According to Wikipedia, X-Prize announced 5 finalists in January 2017: SpaceIL, Moon Express, Synergy Moon, Team Indus and Hakuto, who have secured verified launch contracts with SpaceX, Rocket Lab, Interorbital Systems and ISRO. Other companies, such as the Golden Spike Company and Mission-To-The-Moon that failed to secure launch contracts are no longer in the competition.

Four months after the LRO images were released, NASA produced a document titled; *"NASA's Recommendations to Space-Faring Entities: How to Protect and Preserve the Historic and Scientific Value of U.S. Government Lunar Artifacts."* The document states:

*"NASA recognises. . . space-faring commercial enterprises . . are on the verge of landing spacecraft on the surface of the Moon. Representatives of commercial enterprises have contacted NASA seeking guidance for approaching U.S. Government space assets on the lunar surface."* [38] This document recommends that a 2 Km exclusion zone should be placed around all manned and unmanned landing sites on the Moon, ostensibly to protect them from space tourism! Considering the paucity of evidence that the real technological difficulties were ever overcome,

can we really trust commercial enterprises that claim to be *on the verge of landing spacecraft on the Moon?*

NASA seems to have proposed an exclusion zone and no-fly zone around all lunar sites in response to a commercial race sponsored by Google. The 5 finalists presumably believe that any pictures received back from their lunar robot/rover will indeed be coming from the surface of the Moon, but it may never be possible to independently verify this, and they will presumably comply with NASA's exclusion zone, so nothing will have been proven. Who's protecting whom, and from what?

All the engineers and designers competing for the Google Lunar X-Prize must be relying on NASA data to determine the design parameters of their lunar robots and rovers, but once their robot/rover has disappeared from sight atop a rocket, they will have no way of proving if any digital images they receive back are actually coming from the lunar surface or not. Signals can be relayed via satellites and orbiters to create the illusion that they originated on the Moon or any other celestial body. Similar tricks can be used to create the illusion that signals are returning from the Mars landers and rovers, when they may not be on Mars at all.

Contrary to the usual progression of scientific discovery, the list of unanswered questions about the Apollo missions has grown steadily longer since 1969. The first time a real Saturn 5 rocket was used after the Apollo missions, the vibrations were so severe that the Skylab payload was seriously damaged, so how were all those smooth, trouble-free Apollo launches actually achieved? The lunar lander was still uncontrollable less than 12 months before Apollo 11, and yet apparently performed flawlessly on the Moon. NASA have never satisfactorily explained how the astronauts avoided being cooked alive by the $100^0$C+ temperatures on the lunar surface, or how the landers appear to have landed without creating a blast crater, or why the deafening roar of the ascent engine is absent from voice recordings during lunar take-off, or why the ill-fated Apollo 13 "mission" would have had to land in pitch darkness if it had actually reached the Moon at the planned time; a planning error so basic that it suggests someone knew Apollo 13 would not be going anywhere near the Moon.

# THE RUSSIANS

In spite of this growing catalogue of errors of omission and commission, many still have complete faith in the Apollo story because *the Russians would have known the truth*. Maybe they did know the true extent of American progress, but does that automatically mean they would have blown the whistle?  Since the end of World War 2, the Russians have been portrayed fairly unremittingly as the unscrupulous, untrustworthy bear of world politics, and yet we assume they have been completely open and have misled no one about their own space programme. We trust them when it suits us, and distrust them when it doesn't, it seems. Since the fall of the Soviet Union, more details about the space race have emerged, and the Russian story now has almost as many holes as the Apollo story.

In his book; *One Small Step*, Gerhard Wisnewski  highlights just some of the gaps in the Russian space story. During the Soviet era, the Russians had complete control of their press, so it was not difficult to exaggerate their achievements and conceal their failures. This economy with the truth began with the early unmanned missions. Quoting *Mission Mond;*

*"When a successful entry into an orbit was achieved, the probe was given the name Luna plus a running number. But when a rocket crashed during launch or soon after, it remained without an official name. If the launch was successful but the probe failed to leave the Earth's gravity it*

*was officially included as a satellite in the sequence of countless Sputnik or Cosmos launches."* [39]

According to Wisnewski and other researchers, this mercenary attitude also extended to their later manned flights. *Pravda* confirmed this in 2001:

*"Gagarin was not the first cosmonaut . . .Three Soviet pilots died in attempts to conquer space before Gagarin's famous space flight, reported Mikhail Rudenko, senior engineer-experimenter with Experimental Design Office 456 (located at Khimki, in the Moscow region). According to Rudenko, spacecraft with pilots Ledovskikh, Shaborin and Mitkov at the controls had been launched from the Kapustin Yar cosmodrome (in the Astrakhan region) in 1957, 1958 and 1959."* [40]

This may explain some of the disturbing radio transmissions picked up by amateur radio enthusiasts during these years, notably the Judica-Cordiglia brothers in Turin who received considerable media coverage at the time. In November 1960, the Italian brothers picked up an "SOS to the entire world" in Morse code, with a Doppler shift that suggested the spacecraft was travelling away from the Earth. In February 1961, they picked up the *"racing beat of an over-exerted heart (the hearts of all astronauts are monitored automatically) and sounds of laboured breathing."* [41] And in May 1961, they heard a female Russian voice saying: *"Am I going to crash?.. Yes..Yes..I feel hot!. I feel hot!.. I will re-enter!.. I will re-enter!.."* [42] This was only weeks after Gagarin's apparent orbital trip, and over two years *before* Valentina Tereshkova claimed the title of first woman in space with her June 1963 Vostok 6 flight.

These reports, along with similar reports from other radio enthusiasts and *Pravda's* frank admission, could not contrast more sharply with the story of Uri Gagarin's seemingly trouble-free orbit in April 1961. The Russians claim to have suddenly resolved all their problems in a few months in early '61, much as the Americans claim to have done 8 years later. If radio amateurs around the world were aware of Russia's dirty space secrets, we can be certain American intelligence was also aware, so Russian silence would have been easily secured when Kennedy decided to raise the stakes.

Wisnewski has shown that the Gagarin story does not stand up to close scrutiny. When he died in 1968, Gagarin still only had 75 hours of jet pilot experience in his log book. This means that, by military standards, he was still only a trainee jet pilot. In fact, he died at the controls of a MiG 15 jet, with his instructor next to him when he misjudged a flat figure-eight manoeuvre; an elementary mistake, and that was 7 years *after* his alleged orbital flight.[43] The idea that the Soviets would have placed their national pride in the hands of a trainee like Gagarin is laughable. Wisnewski has carefully plotted the progress of Gagarin's Vostok 1 capsule, and found that his voice transmissions were ridiculously vague, and bear no relation to his geographical position during the flight [44] – it's quite possible that the only passenger on Vostok 1 was a tape recorder. Gagarin himself parachuted back to Earth only a few miles from his training ground; an extremely unlikely feat at the end of an essentially uncontrolled spaceflight. It's likely that Gagarin was little more than a photogenic poster boy for the Soviet space programme.

In 2013, perhaps in response to the growing cynicism about Gagarin, Russia Today published an article by Aleksey Leonov suggesting that Gagarin's MiG was sent into a spin by an Su-15 fighter that passed by at a height of only 500m after being cleared to overfly the airfield at 10,000m (32,800 ft)[45]. Apart from the lack of evidence and sheer unlikeliness of this story, Aleksey Leonov has good reason to want to shore up the official version of Soviet space exploration. Though Leonov was feted for performing the first ever spacewalk in 1965, several authors, starting with Peter McWilliams, have suggested that the video was faked in a studio. In *NASA Mooned America*, Ralph Rene easily showed that Michael Collins' photo of his 1966 Gemini 10 spacewalk was simply cut and pasted from a zero-G jet training flight.[46] If Gagarin's flight was a propaganda stunt and the Americans were still faking spacewalk photos in '66, a year after Ed White had apparently completed America's first spacewalk, then we are entitled to be cynical about Leonov's spacewalk and his motives for attempting to defend Gagarin.

The real unsung heroes of the Soviet space race were cosmonauts like Valentin Bondarenko and Vladimir Ilyushin, son of Sergei Ilyushin, the aerospace engineer. Bondarenko and Ilyushin had both suffered serious injuries in suborbital flights in the weeks preceding Gagarin's alleged flight.[47] According to Istvan Nemere, Bondarenko was rushed to a Moscow hospital after being very badly burned.[48] The Russians claimed this was the result of an accident in an oxygen chamber, but they have never used pure oxygen in their spacecraft – it's far more likely that Bondarenko had been burned alive in an uncontrolled re-entry.

At the time of Gagarin's alleged flight, Russia's most famous test pilot, Vladimir Ilyushin, was in hospital in China, ostensibly recovering from a car accident. Elliot Haimoff tracked Ilyushin down for his *Cosmonaut Coverup*[49] documentary and believes that Ilyushin had actually crash landed in China after a serious electrical malfunction during an attempted orbital flight. This makes far more sense – Russian medical facilities were perfectly adequate for treating car crash injuries. Haimoff makes the point that, under the Khrushchev regime, failure meant banishment to a Siberian labour camp. After Ilyushin's embarrassing failure, the chief Soviet rocket engineer, Sergey Korolyov would have known that he needed a big success to save his own neck, and only five days later Gagarin's successful orbit was announced, with no supporting photos, whilst Khrushchev was on holiday! Was this the moment that Korolyov and his team took the Soviet space programme into the "black"?[50] Jock Bruce Gardyne thought so, and expressed his misgivings in a Daily Telegraph article a few years later: "Was Gagarin Russia's answer to the Piltdown Man?"[51]

This also suggests that the Chinese would have been well aware of the disparity between the truth and the propaganda of the Soviet space programme, which in turn might explain why the Chinese National Space Administration has been able to join the great space propaganda game with its 2013 Chang'e – 3 lander / Yutu rover mission to the Moon. Why they would want to join the game is, of course, an interesting question in itself. Is it unreasonable to suggest that a few scientists within the Chinese National Space Administration may not have the best interests of their own citizens at heart?

# CUI BONO?

Whilst Russia's rocket scientists may have put a tape recorder into orbit and released some fake news to save their own necks, it is the central thesis of this book that this deception has been exploited for altogether more sinister long-term motives by small groups of administrators and scientists at NASA, ESA, CNSA and Roscosmos who are well aware of the limitations of rocket technology, and are exploiting public and politicians alike for their paymasters within the military-industrial complex[52]. Joseph Farrell has looked closely at NASA's origins, and in the preface to his book, *The Philosopher's Stone* he ventures to suggest that space may not be quite what it seems:

". . . There would indeed seem to be adumbrations of confirmations of ancient esoteric views of the physical medium, and that shadowy groups in the contemporary world are intent upon recovering that lost science, implementing the whole range of technologies that it implies, and monopolizing it for themselves. . . . And that, interestingly enough, will lead us in turn, once again, to NASA and NASA's Nazis." [53]

In *The Hunt for Zero Point,* Nick Cook noted that the 1,500 German scientists recruited under the Office of Strategic Services' Operation Paperclip brought something more dangerous than rocket science with them:

"The Nazis developed a unique approach to science and engineering quite separate from the rest of the world, because their ideology, unrestrained as it was, supported a wholly different way of doing things . . . The trouble was, when the Americans took it all home with them

42

they found out, too late, that it came infected with a virus. You take the science on, you take on aspects of the ideology as well." [54]

By a strange twist of fate, the virus that Nick Cook speaks of seems to have found a particularly susceptible host organism in the fledgling OSS/CIA and NASA. In his book *Dark Mission; The Secret History of NASA*, Richard Hoagland depicts an "Organization chart showing Masons, SS members and "magicians" in key positions of power all throughout NASA in the 1960s. Everybody who was anybody at the Agency, from the director on down, was a member of one of these three secret cults." [55]

The Masons were represented by James Webb, the NASA administrator, and Kenneth Kleinknecht who was a director of the Mercury, Gemini and Apollo projects. The Masons were also well represented amongst the astronauts – by 1969 the list included Buzz Aldrin, Gordon Cooper, Donn Eisle, Walter Schirra, Tom Stafford, Ed Mitchell and Paul Weitz.

The "magicians" were led by Jack Parsons at JPL. Parsons was another deeply imbalanced individual – he actually believed he was the antichrist! Aleister Crowley wanted him to lead his amoral Thelemite religion, which appears to be some form of neo-satanism. The most visible Nazis, though technically ex-Nazis, were Wernher von Braun, Kurt Debus and Humbertus Strughold. The nascent American space programme seems to have been endowed with the technical means, the inhuman motive and the Masonic opportunity to deceive us all.

Whilst Richard Hoagland's Dark Mission book starts correctly by stating that *"The NASA we've known for over 50 years has been a lie"*, he then assumes that the only possible motive for lying is to conceal photographic evidence of extraterrestrial archaeology from the public! Hoagland has done an excellent job of revealing some of NASA's Masons, magicians and Nazis, but then imposes his own theories about transparent glass skyscrapers on the Moon and the "face on Mars" as his explanation for NASA's duplicitous nature. So some of the most damning evidence against NASA will be dismissed out-of-hand by being associated with Hoagland's wild theories. Hoagland does not, for a second consider the possibility that entire sets of photos have been faked even though Oleg Oleynik has proved this is the case. So another opportunity to do some real damage to the NASA PR machine may have been missed. Was this by accident or design?

If the Apollo missions were faked, then we have to consider the possibility that coercive MK Ultra-style techniques may have been used on at least some of the astronauts and other NASA personnel. Within the MK Ultra programmes, a deeply disturbing, inhuman influence is again perceivable. Who would have been so lacking in empathy as to be able to inflict extreme pain whilst under drugs and/or hypnosis, just to gain psychological control of another individual? Buzz Aldrin was physically sick when pressed in public to describe what it was like to walk on the moon – a classic sign of trauma-based hypnotic conditioning. When Mike Siegel asked Gordon Cooper about the Space Kids training project on Coast to Coast Radio, Cooper's reply was revealing:

"The space kids were children with exceptional mental abilities run through a kind of MK programme, like the things that are coming out now." [56]

If some of the astronauts had false memories implanted under deep hypnosis, others show all the signs of being fully conscious of their lies. Peter Hyatt is a professional American Statement Analyst who has provided vital evidence about witness reliability in hundreds of court cases just by examining the psychology and grammar of their responses under questioning . When witnesses or defendants lie, their mind must censor and insert artificial information in a very short space of time. This interrupts their normal cognitive processes and choice of words, so their speech patterns change. In 2017, Richard D Hall asked Peter Hyatt to analyse Patrick Moore's 1970 BBC TV interview with Neil Armstrong. The full interview, along with Hyatt's analysis and Richard D Hall's comments can be viewed on Youtube or the Richplanet.net website by searching for "Analysing The Astronauts". Here are some quotes from

Hyatt's analysis, reproduced with Richard D Hall's kind permission. The words of the original interview are in **bold** text, and Hyatt's comments in italics[57];

*(P. Hyatt) The context is the Lunar landing. This was a unique, dramatic and historical event. The expectation of truth, therefore is the following linguistic formula for reliability:*

1. *The Pronoun "I"*
2. *Past Tense Verbs*
3. *Sensory description*

**Patrick Moore: "Could you tell us something about what the sky actually looks like from the Moon?"**

**Neil Armstrong: "The sky is erm a deep black, err, when viewed from the Moon as it is when viewed from er cislunar space, the space between the Earth and the Moon."**

*(P. Hyatt) Given the unique experience of being on the Moon, we first note that the subject does not begin his answer with the pronoun "I." In analysis, this reduces reliability. Given the context of unique experience, the pronoun "I" would have shown the psychological strength of experiential memory. It's absence is noted.*

*Next, we note the use of passive voice with "when viewed from the Moon." Passive voice removes the subject, himself, personally from the statement. The use of passivity is found in concealing identity and/or responsibility in statements. . . With such a unique and unusual event, we expect not only a strong use of the pronoun "I" but of distinct sensory detail: what his eyes experienced, including emotional impact. This is common among those who speak from experiential memory and is often used to discern veracity. He has told us it is "deep black" but not that he saw it.*

**Neil Armstrong: *"The, erm, the Earth is the only visible object other than the sun that can be seen although there've been some reports of seeing planets."***

*(P. Hyatt) This is his second sentence after reporting in both passive and universal language. He tells us, in general terms what "you" (universal, unnamed) can know, similar to what would be reported in a textbook. . . There is no linguistic connection here between the subject and experiential language to this point.*

**Neil Armstrong: *"I myself did not see planets from the surface, but I suspect they might er be visible."***

*(P. Hyatt) Since he experienced something highly unique, not only does he report what he did not see, but he feels it necessary to input himself into the sentence, where no such imputation should be needed. Who else would be answering this question, or "not seeing" what he did not see?*

**Patrick Moore: *"What about the sun? Did you see any trace of the corona?"***

**Neil Armstrong: *"No the er glare from the Sun on the helmet visor was too difficult to pick out the corona."***

*(P. Hyatt) Here he says "no", which answers the question, but then continues to avoid personal linguistic connection such as: "No, the glare from the sun on my helmet visor was too difficult for me to pick out the corona." This would have been a statement of personal connection which he has not yet made. Remember, he was asked, "Did you. . .?" with the focus upon himself. He should answer for himself.*

**Neil Armstrong: *". . You can see, er browns er if the Sun is high enough. Apollo 12 for example landed while the Sun was only 5 degrees above the horizon so when they arrived they saw no browns or tans anywhere, only fairly high contrast greys."***

**Patrick Moore, interrupting: "But you did?"**

**Neil Armstrong: "But, Yes I did. The Sun was at 11 degrees and Apollo 12 did also the next day . . ."**

*(P. Hyatt) Here we finally have the subject speaking for himself. When he said, "But yes I did . ." we hold to an expectation that he would now include himself ("I") and tell us the sensory descriptions within personal experiential memory. He does not. He went back to history from his previous answer. Therefore, we do not have the linguistic connection that remains expected.*

**Neil Armstrong: "Yes we had er, some difficulties in perception of, of diffic . . of distance, er for example our TV camera, err, we judged to be from the cockpit of the lunar module only about er 50 to er 60 feet away."**

*(P. Hyatt) He does not speak for himself even in the realm of "perception". This is to address the brain's interpretation of what was seen or experienced. He consistently in the interview tells us what "we" saw, "we" thought, "we" perceived, as well as what "you" saw, and so on. Although many of these topics were likely discussed, he should still be speaking for himself. The use of "we" is most unexpected. We must now consider that if he is not deceptive, why does he have a reason to "join a crowd" even in personal experience and perception.*

*Hyatt concludes: Neil Armstrong does not linguistically connect himself to the lunar landing. This is evident in his consistent 'distancing language' including intuitive pronouns and passivity. . . If I were to take this interview and change the names to unknown, and change words which would no longer indicate the setting (1969 lunar landing), it is likely that analysts would conclude that the subject is not speaking from experiential memory and question if deception is evident. The context is difficult to overcome and we must consider what would cause him to show no experiential memory of such a dramatic and singular historical experience.*

*Lastly, we must consider the inclusion of emotion for the subject in his final answer. This is especially striking because he did not connect emotion to self in his descriptions of what the interviewer alleges Mr Armstrong experiences. (The interviewer linguistically placed Mr Armstrong on the Moon; something Mr Armstrong did not).*

*Mr Armstrong does not here linguistically place himself on the Moon. The refusal of commitment is consistent. There is not one place in the interview where he used the normal linguistic connection to experiential memory.*

Analysing an astronaut's grammar under questioning may not prove that the Moon landings were faked, but the principles of statement analysis are well recognised and widely accepted in court, and Hyatt has applied these principles in hundreds of cases, so his analysis can be taken as very strong evidence that Armstrong was at least lying in this interview. And it's difficult to call Hyatt's objectivity into question as he admitted to Richard D Hall, after analysing Armstrong's interview, that as a patriotic American, he was surprised and disturbed by the implications of his own analysis. Perhaps it was the painful evasiveness of this interview with Patrick Moore that caused Armstrong to refuse interviews for decades afterwards. Buzz Aldrin, Peter Conrad and Edgar Mitchell also struggled with this inability to relate personally to the experience of being on the Moon.

Returning to NASA's dark origins, even Wikipedia is fairly unambiguous about the subject. It currently states (Jan 2017) that:

" . . more than 1,500 scientists, engineers and technicians (many of whom were formerly registered members of the Nazi Party, and some of whom had leadership roles in the Nazi Party) were recruited and brought to the U.S. for government employment from post-Nazi Germany. The primary purpose of Operation Paperclip was for the U.S. to gain a scientific and military advantage in the burgeoning cold war, and later space race between the U.S. and Soviet Union. By comparison, the Soviet Union were even more aggressive in recruiting Germans: during Operation Osoaviakhim, Soviet military units forcibly recruited 2,000 + German specialists to the Soviet Union during one night."

This unseemly grab for German scientific know-how runs counter to the official story of Allied technological superiority at the end of the war and may betray a very uncomfortable truth. Joseph Farrell, Igor Witkowski, Nicholas Goodricke-Clarke and others have amassed plenty of evidence that this haste was motivated by much more than a desire to secure the services of the best German rocket engineers. According to Goodricke-Clarke:

"In 1959 Major Rodolf Lusar, who had worked at the German Patent Office, wrote a lengthy account of the extraordinary variety of missiles, flying bombs and long-range rockets in operational use before the end of the war. He also discussed the flying disks of Schriever, Habermohl and Miethe, who were supported by an Italian physicist called Bellonzo."

Since the end of the war, there has been a steady trickle of evidence that the Germans were well ahead of the allies in many other areas of weapons research, including radar absorbent materials, computers, fuel-air bombs, rotational (torsion) physics, turbines, Schauberger's vortexes, infrared fuses, nuclear fission and fusion devices and even more exotic weaponry such as jet-powered disks[58]. They had produced more than enough enriched Uranium, and if eye-witness accounts can be believed, may even have tested some type of fission weapon on the Eastern front, but did not have a bomber large enough to deliver their new weapon. Recently declassified files from the National Archive in Washington (APO696) suggest that the Germans tested a rudimentary warhead in October 1944 near Ludwigslust[59].

At this point, just before we descend into sci-fi paranoia and blame everything on Herr Doktor Nine in his secret bunker, we need to know just how far these ground-breaking technologies may have progressed behind closed doors, keeping in mind the military imperative to control and exploit technology, rather than share it. Farrell believes that Gabriel Kron's tensor analysis was already leading German physics in unexpected directions in the 1930s[60]. Kron was a pragmatic electrical engineer who understood that even the equations in his own prize-winning 1935 paper on "Non-Reimannian Dynamics of Rotating Electrical Machinery" were only *symbolic;* useful stepping-stones, unlike Einstein who regarded maths as *reality.* In *Secrets of The Unified Field,* Farrell writes:

"It is therefore in the years leading up to World War Two that we see what has become a permanent feature in what had hitherto been a more or less open and free discipline, as physics itself split into two branches: that for the masses in a kind of "public consumption" physics intentionally designed to lead to "dead ends", and that for the secret scientists, technicians and engineers, the wizards in their black projects temples." [61]

President Eisenhower recognised that military research was a threat to the rightful development of science and could unleash forces that even the world's greatest democracy might not be able to control. He coined the phrase "military-industrial complex" to describe the scientific-technological elite and realised that he would only get one opportunity to warn us about this growing enemy within. In his farewell address in January 1961, he warned:

"In the councils of government, we must guard against the acquisition of unwarranted influence, whether sought or unsought, by the military-industrial complex. The potential for the disastrous rise of misplaced power exists and will persist. We must never let the weight of this combination endanger our liberties or democratic processes. We should take nothing for granted. Only an alert and knowledgeable citizenry can compel the proper meshing of the huge industrial and military machinery of defence with our peaceful methods and goals, so that security and liberty may prosper together . . . The prospect of domination of the nation's scholars by Federal employment, project allocation, and the power of money is ever present and is gravely to be regarded." [62] With the benefit of hindsight, it looks likely that President Kennedy may have paid with his life for threatening these same vested interests only three years after Eisenhower's warning.

It is slowly becoming apparent that research in physics, chemistry and the other natural sciences progressed in many interesting directions in Germany in the '30s and '40s. This flourishing of the physical sciences under far right wing ideology may not be entirely coincidental. The separation of thought from feeling that is necessary for reductionist scientific reasoning can become brutal inhumanity when taken to the extreme. This cold, controlling mentality is a form of imbalance that has appeared in many guises and will haunt humanity for millennia to come.

In Rudolf Steiner's Anthroposophy, this imbalance can take two forms; the right wing and the left wing of thinking; the Ahrimanic and the luciferic. Ahrimanic thinking focusses on selfish, individual needs, leading to endless war, and animalistic *survival of the fittest*, whereas Luciferic thinking completely subjugates individual needs "for the greater good". But both of these paths lead ultimately to loss of that most precious human commodity: free will. We only find our humanity in the centre, by exercising our own free will whilst respecting that of others.

The obsessive desire for power over others has always been around and has exerted a long term influence on the development of scientific thinking precisely *because* of the success of science, though this is not immediately obvious. One of the attractions of modern, reductionist physical science is that, by creating the impression that consciousness is of no real consequence, we feel absolved from our responsibility to monitor our own motives, our own state of consciousness, and to consider the morality of our actions. But we can only live in that comfortable, doubt-free world as long as we stick to the material paradigm as it is currently defined. By constantly reassuring us that our preconceptions are correct, we can be easily persuaded that there is nothing modern scientists cannot understand, that questioning the status quo is misguided and futile. When science expands to include our own thinking, our own consciousness in the equation, however, we re-enter the uncomfortable realm of self-examination and self-discipline and have to fall back on our moral compasses for guidance.

Scientific knowledge may be neither good nor evil, but it can be put to either good or evil uses, so morality is inextricably linked to science and technology. He who controls mainstream science (or exactly which technologies are publically available) has a degree of control over our thinking. *The fantasy of scientific omniscience*[63], to use Rupert Sheldrake's phrase, has existed since Francis Bacon's time. The other side of the coin - the impetus to divert the scientific consensus just enough to conceal and exploit new technology - has existed just as long. The Aetheraware.org website asks the unthinkable: "Are these failings of Western science deliberate or accidental? Is this an issue of integrity or ignorance?" To assume that such motives do not exist is naïve, as we found to our cost in the twentieth century.

The right wing megalomania of the last century did not disappear in 1945. It has emerged in many forms in the past and, though it may have been driven underground, it will always try to use cutting-edge science to gain the advantage; to exploit the rest of humanity. We may not think of it as such, but science is really a spiritual battleground, complete with all the propaganda and espionage of any long-running war. And as with any war, hidden financial interests play a much larger role than is immediately apparent, as Eisenhower warned. The battle for control of the scientific high ground is ongoing, and the stakes could not be higher.

# THE DEAD UNIVERSE

The modern scientific mindset analyses the matter and energy from which the observable universe is composed, and has provided undeniably astonishing technological advances. Within this strictly materialist paradigm, all matter is composed of subatomic particles that formed within minutes of a Big Bang, all life has arisen by chance from that matter and consciousness is just an electrical epiphenomenon of the brain; an illusion. Within this deterministic model, there is no room for free will – human beings, including all our thoughts and feelings, are merely the random consequence of the laws of physics. We are just "lumbering robots", to use Richard Dawkins' phrase. This habit of pushing all the hardest philosophical questions back to the dawn of time, and wrapping them up in some equations, was brilliantly captured by Terence McKenna in one phrase:    "Give us one free miracle, and we'll explain the rest." [64]

This mechanistic view is very successful when analysing and utilising dead matter, but is not quite so successful when applied to organic life, and assumes that consciousness itself is of no real consequence in the grand scheme of things. The relentless march of technological progress since the industrial revolution has ensured that faith in this mechanistic model has spread globally, and has become a badge of honour for well-educated people around the world. But, surprisingly for a strictly rational endeavour, this outlook contains many unprovable assumptions, and scientific conclusions can never be any more solid than these initial assumptions. Dr Edi Bilimoria, a highly experienced engineer, is aware of the dangers of extrapolating from unproven assumptions:

"You can build an Eiffel Tower of logic on very shaky sands. And the logic and the superstructure can be impregnable but it will topple over if your fundamental assumptions are shaky." [65]

Many of the conclusions of modern science about black holes, the expanding universe, dark matter and gravity waves are simply the inevitable consequence of assumptions that have been absorbed into the mechanistic model without ever being proven. Black holes, dark matter and the Higgs boson are the theoretical consequences of projecting our Earthly understanding of gravity outwards into the universe, and any evidence for their existence, however tenuous, is seized upon by the self-perpetuating scientific establishment.

Rupert Sheldrake set out to re-examine the assumptions that are inherent within the modern scientific view in his book *The Science Delusion*[66]. Though billed as a riposte to Dawkins' book *The God Delusion,* it was not Sheldrake's intention to denigrate the scientific method, but merely to point out that these inherent assumptions have slowly solidified into dogmas that are now strangling the spirit of open-minded scientific enquiry. Sheldrake has defined this modern scientific creed in ten core beliefs:

1. Everything is essentially mechanical, including animals and humans.
2. All matter is unconscious - even human consciousness is an illusion.
3. The total amount of matter and energy is always the same (except for the Big Bang).
4. The laws of nature are fixed.

5   Nature is purposeless.

6   All biological inheritance is material, carried in the genetic material, DNA.

7   Minds are inside heads and are nothing but the activities of brains.

8   Memories are stored as material traces in brains and are wiped out at death.

9   Unexplained phenomena like telepathy are illusory.

10  Mechanistic medicine is the only kind that really works.

Rupert Sheldrake examined each of these beliefs in detail, and found that they are not only unproven, there is sound evidence that some of them are just plain wrong. The first two points are really philosophical assumptions. Many scientifically minded people assert that consciousness must be illusory, which means free will does not really exist, but when they finish work, they enjoy exercising that free will as much as anyone else! Even Francis Crick, the co-discoverer of DNA had to admit that the mechanistic view of biological life, this "astonishing hypothesis", flies in the face of our own inner experience.

Points 3 and 4 form the bedrock of modern cosmology, but that bedrock keeps splitting along old fault-lines. Newtonian gravity was found to be too weak to hold galaxies together, so invisible dark matter had to be invented to hold the universe together, but then in the 1990s the universe appeared to be expanding too quickly, so anti-gravitational dark energy had to be invented to explain supernovas. The idea that anti-gravity may exist here on Earth is universally dismissed in academia, and yet anti-gravitational dark energy is used to explain the behaviour of distant supernovae. The universal gravitational constant, big G, seems to get less constant the more accurately we measure it, which suggests that it may not be constant at all. Between 1973 and 2010, it varied by over 1% [67]. In recent years it has been found that the value of another "constant", the fine structure constant, seems to depend on which direction you point your telescope [68].

An article titled *Cosmic Inflation Theory Faces Challenges* posed some long overdue questions in the February 2017 edition of Scientific American;

" . . Yet even now, the cosmology community has not taken a cold, hard look at the big bang inflationary theory or paid significant attention to critics who question whether inflation happened."[69]

The article prompted a response from a group of 33 physicists, including Stephen Hawking, who accused Scientific American of dismissing their research, and that of "a substantial contingent of the scientific community". The argument centred around voids in the cosmic microwave background (CMB) found by the Planck satellite, which have been cited as evidence for the existence of parallel universes!

Stephen Hawking, Michio Kaku and Neil deGrasse Tyson believe we should adhere to mathematical theories about parallel universes rather than question the big bang theory, even though Australian mathematician Steve Crothers has already proved that the mathematical assumptions within Hawking's work are completely contradictory, which means Hawking's conclusions are worthless. Is this an example of scientific "consensus" being reached by peer review, or simply by bullying? Like so many before him, Steve Crothers' reward for having the temerity to re-examine the fundamentals of modern cosmology was the end of his academic career, even though this is completely contrary to the spirit of scientific enquiry. This argument has been covered in more detail in the Thunderbolts Project video; *More Big Problems for Big Bang*[70].

Whilst researching *The Science Delusion,* Sheldrake visited the Head of Metrology at the National Physical Laboratory in London to ask how the official value for the speed of light was determined, as there have been slight variations in its value. Between 1928 and 1945, its value fell by about 20 Km/s around the world, even though relativity dictates that it should be a constant. The answers he received were extremely revealing, as he recounts in his Youtube video; *Rupert Sheldrake – The Science Delusion Banned TED talk* [71]:

R.S. – "What do you make of this drop in the speed of light between 1928 and 1945?"

Dr P. - "Oh dear, you've uncovered the most embarrassing incident in the history of our science."

R.S. – "Could the speed of light have actually dropped?"

Dr P. – "No, of course it couldn't have actually dropped – it's a constant."

R.S. – "Well how do you explain everyone finding it going more slowly during that period? Is it because they were fudging their results?"

Dr P. – "We don't like to use the word fudge."

R.S. – "What would you prefer?"

Dr P. – "We prefer to call it intellectual phase locking."

R.S. – "How do you know it's not still being fudged?"

Dr P. – "We solved the problem. We fixed the speed of light by definition in 1972."

R.S. – "But it might still change."

Dr P. – "Yes, but we'd never know it, as we've defined the meter in terms of the speed of light."

So the scientific establishment have fixed the speed of light at a constant value because, according to Einstein's relativity, it must be a constant! Propping up Einstein's relativity has now become more important than actual observation of the real world over long periods. Dr Edi Bilimoria confirms that some scientists have become the high priests of a new religion, deciding amongst themselves what the rest of us should be told to believe:

"Modern science has done Einstein a great disservice, for a start, in turning "the speed of light is constant" almost into a religious cult. This is nonsense. The speed of light is not constant. There is a lot of evidence, experimental evidence, to show it is not constant. It was made constant in order to make the results of Michelson-Morley fit Relativity." [72]

Having been a biochemist and cell biologist at Cambridge, Sheldrake is well qualified to examine points 5 and 6 on his list, and once again the mechanistic view was found wanting. In June 2000, President Clinton heralded the printing of the first draft of the Human Genome. Mechanistic biologists proclaimed the dawning of a new age of genetic reprogramming of the "human machine". One over-excited editor of *Nature* claimed that genomics . . .

". . .will allow us to fashion the human form into any conceivable shape. We will have extra limbs, if we want them, and maybe even wings to fly." [73]

In reality, the Human Genome Project, despite the expenditure of more than $100 billion, has done little more than highlight the missing heritability problem. To quote Sheldrake:

"In practice, the predictive value of human genomes turned out to be small, in some cases less than that achieved with a measuring tape. Tall parents tend to have tall children, and short parents short children. By measuring the height of parents, their children's heights can be predicted with 80 to 90% accuracy. In other words, height is 80 to 90% heritable. Recent "genome-wide association studies" compared the genomes of 30,000 people and identified about 50 genes associated with tallness or shortness. To everyone's surprise, taken together, these genes accounted for only about 5% of the inheritance of height. In other words, the "height" genes did *not* account for 75 to 85% of the heritability of height. Most of the heritability was missing." [74] It is slowly becoming apparent that genes are not the computer software of the human organism, as biologists have assumed since the discovery of DNA.

Sheldrake uses points 7-10 to examine psychic phenomena in humans and animals, backed up by research using double-blind methods, and uses his own ideas about *morphic fields* to explain the non-physical nature of memory and consciousness.

# THE GHOST IN THE MACHINE

Whilst inanimate matter behaves in predictable, mechanical ways, should we really accept that organic life is governed by the laws of physics and chemistry alone? The philosophical conundrum that can never be answered by this mechanistic outlook is; how can consciousness arise from unconscious, inanimate matter? Where is the ghost within the human machine? As Sheldrake puts it:

"The little man, or homunculus, inside the brain remained a common way of thinking about the relation of body and mind, but the metaphor moved with the times and adapted to new technologies. In the mid-twentieth century the homunculus was usually a telephone operator in the telephone exchange of the brain, and he saw projected images of the external world as if he were in a cinema, as in a book published in 1949 called *The Secret of Life: The Human Machine and How it Works. . . .* The ghosts in the machine were implicit rather than explicit, but obviously this was no explanation at all because the little men inside brains would themselves have to have little men inside their brains, and so on in an infinite regress." [75]

This problem, the so-called *hard problem* of philosophy has always bedevilled objective, scientific thought, and has prompted some of the greatest minds of the 20th century, including Werner Heisenberg, to ask whether consciousness could be an inherent property of matter, rather than presuming that matter is unconscious, and perpetually chasing the *ghost in the machine*. This idea, also called panpsychism, has been championed in recent years by philosophers like Galen Strawson, and harks back to a much more traditional, spiritual worldview. Though it is the polar opposite of the prevailing view within scientific academia, there is actually nothing irrational about starting from this point. Modern science assumes that consciousness has gradually evolved from matter, but it is *equally valid* to assume that matter has evolved from consciousness. Most scientifically minded people refuse to take this step on the grounds that we cannot be objective about our own consciousness, so this can never be the subject of rational scientific discourse. But I can be objective about your consciousness and vice versa, so consciousness *can* be the subject of rational analysis.

If matter has somehow evolved from consciousness, how could something so endlessly complex, beautiful and intricate as the physical world have possibly evolved from something as numinous and ill-defined as consciousness or spirit? This question seems to lead us away from the founding (materialist) principles of modern science, but it actually takes us right back to Plato, who believed that ideas are eternal and can even have definite structure, like the platonic solids.

H.P.Blavatsky tried to convey the ancient Tibetan Buddhist understanding of the evolution of solid matter over aeons of time in her books *Isis Unveiled* and *The Secret Doctrine*, but it was Rudolf Steiner who put her Theosophical view on a much more objective, rational footing from 1904, now published under the title *An Outline of Esoteric Science* [76]. This work describes the parallel evolution of matter *and* consciousness through warm, gaseous and liquid phases in the distant past before independent consciousness and solid matter appeared. This understanding of the sequential development of solid matter may ultimately be used to shed light on the inverse relationship between the structure of the atom and the structure of consciousness. The idea that consciousness may have a complex, causal structure is anathema to modern science, but is entirely appropriate within this much wider historical context.

In recent years, quantum physicists have tried to explore the centre ground between matter and consciousness, but we are still left with a very profound question: What *are* the quanta of quantum physics? Phrases like quantum consciousness have become very fashionable but are really just new window-dressing for the same old speculation about the nature of the "ghost in the machine". Is thinking, in some sense, a numerical (but not abstract mathematical) process?

To escape from philosophical tail-chasing, consciousness must be non-material, but your consciousness and mine seem to be governed by the same set of "rules", and the simplest non-material things that follow strictly determined rules are numbers themselves. If consciousness functions consistently from one individual to another, as seems to be the case, then the Pythagorean dictum "All is number" should be applied to consciousness as well as matter, but this would have to occur within a non-deterministic framework, otherwise there would be no "room" for us to exercise the free will we self-evidently possess.

The very fact that modern science can be delineated by a set of dogmatic beliefs, when the function of science is to replace belief with independently verifiable knowledge, does not augur well for the conclusions of modern science. When deterministic thinking was at its zenith in the late 19th century, Lord Kelvin is supposed to have said "There is nothing new to be discovered in physics now. All that remains is more and more precise measurement."

In 1927, Heisenberg's Uncertainty Principle seriously undermined many Victorian scientific certainties, but the old determinism seems to have slowly absorbed and regrouped around quantum physics. Though the position of one particle may be indeterminate, the statistical distribution of particles can still be predicted, so the behaviour of large numbers of particles is still essentially deterministic. We may not be able to predict the behaviour of one swallow at any given moment, but the migratory path of a flock of swallows is still predictable. Quantum physics has spawned a plethora of theories about the entanglement of matter and consciousness, even though the majority of scientists still seem to be in denial about the existence of their own free will!

The Copenhagen Interpretation of the Uncertainty Principle took quantum physics into the unprovable and unscientific realm of endless parallel universes. This has also been called the "Shut up and calculate approach" as it allows us to make calculations about subatomic particles but does not allow us to ask meaningful questions about those subatomic interactions. Writing in his 1997 book *The End of Science,* John Horgan, senior science writer at Scientific American showed that Lord Kelvin's mechanistic outlook has, once again, become the default position of the scientific establishment:

"If one believes in science, one must accept the possibility – even the probability – that the great era of scientific discovery is over. By science I mean not applied science, but science at its purest and greatest, the primordial human quest to understand the universe and our place in it. Further research may yield no more revelations or revolutions, but only incremental, diminishing returns." [77]

This depressing statement could only come from someone who has unquestioningly accepted all the existing scientific doctrines. If all the research grants currently controlled by such blinkered minds were used to re-examine existing scientific dogma, academic science could be revivified by the spirit of genuine scientific enquiry. In the meantime, vast research budgets are being consumed by experiments that are so expensive they may never be independently verified, which means they are of limited value. The statistical proof of the existence of the Higgs boson (you know what they say about statistics) and the apparent detection of gravity waves[78] are but two recent examples of hugely expensive experiments that appear to support the established material view, but do not stand up well to close scrutiny.

In *Rudolf Steiner and The Atom*, Keith Francis questions the validity of statistical analysis; "If you did the experiment with 6,000 dice, however, you might justly expect that each number will turn up close to 1/6 of the time. If this doesn't happen, you are more likely to suspect that there is something wrong with the dice than that there is something wrong with the laws of probability. This may give us the uneasy feeling that the laws of probability are not subject to experimental verification." [79]

The combination of commercial funding and this climate of unquestioning academic conformity has distorted some areas of science, particularly in the biological sciences, to the point that some results are no longer reproducible. If a drug company funds ten different trials of a new drug, and only one of those trials shows positive results, then they will only publish the results of the positive trial, even though the drug may be doing more harm than good. The corporate ownership of scientific results is counter to the spirit of scientific enquiry and is distorting the development of science itself. In a Youtube interview titled "Physicalism is regressing", recorded 1/12/2016, Rupert Sheldrake revealed just how bad this problem has become;

"It turns out a great deal of mainstream scientific research is not replicable, that there's been what are now called questionable research practices throughout the scientific world for a long time now. . . The most questionable aspect, most scientists have known about this for years but thought it wasn't important, is that scientists may only publish about 5 or 10% of their data, and they select what they publish. The rest remains in the privacy of their file drawers, so obviously, if you only select 5 or 10% of your income or expenditure to present to the Inland Revenue, then you might present the 5 or 10% that render you least liable for tax, and clearly there's a scope for tremendous distortion. And two years ago, one of the main drug companies commissioned a replication of the top 50 papers in biomedical science, and 45 turned out to be not replicable – ninety percent." [80]

The staggering scale of this problem was revealed in articles in *The Scientist* magazine[81] (18/12/2012), in *Nature* in May 2016[82] (*1,500 Scientists lift the Lid on Reproducibility),* and in *Nexus* magazine in June 2017 (*Reliability of Cancer Studies Put to Test).*

In an article titled *The Power of Useless* in *New Scientist* (18/3/2017), Simon Ings wrote about the damaging effect of commercial interests on research:

"The administrative burdens and stultifying oversight structures throttling today's scholars come not from Soviet-style central planning, but from the application of market principles . . . if our ingenious, post-war market solution to the totalitarian nightmare of the 1940s has itself turned out to be a great vampire squid wrapped around the face of humanity (as journalist Matt Taibbi once described investment bank Goldman Sachs), where have we left to go?"

Where has science left to go, indeed? If the unquestioning, commercially-enforced acceptance of current dogma persists, then Lord Kelvin and John Horgan's predictions will prove correct; further research will yield only incremental, diminishing returns.

The self-evident existence of our own free will seems to contradict the most basic assumptions of modern science, yet we cannot honestly deny our own capacity for independent thought and action. The constitution of our own inner being tells us that some of the assumptions of science are flawed. But how can our own inner constitution possibly shed any light on the physical world around us? What is the way forward? Which scientific babies have been thrown out with the proverbial bathwater over the past few hundred years?

# THE FUTURE IN THE PAST

The Copernican revolution marked the separation of independent thought from Church dogma. In his book *De Revolutionibus Orbium Coelestium*, first published in 1543, Nicolaus Copernicus revived and elaborated on the heliocentric ideas of Philolaus and Aristarchus from the third and fourth centuries BC. Giordano Bruno preached the heliocentric gospel to the great and the good from Rome to Oxford, and paid with his life in 1600. Galileo used his telescope to provide solid evidence that the Earth goes round the Sun, and was lucky to escape the same fate as Bruno. Kepler modified the circular planetary orbits to elliptical ones and Newton proposed an inverse square gravitational law to hold the planets in orbit, and so the foundations of modern astronomy and cosmology were laid.

Newton's *Principia* drew parallels between the force of gravity here, on Earth, and the forces that keep the planets in orbit, and so it became acceptable to extrapolate from our earthly experience; to use our understanding of mechanics and physics to make sense of the whole universe. Before Newton, it had been assumed that the laws of the Earthly realm and the Heavenly realms were entirely separate. Suddenly, the heavens seemed to be accessible to ordinary, free-thinking mortals, not just the preserve of an educated elite.

But Newton never claimed to understand the mechanism of gravitational attraction, he only found a way to *describe* the apparent variation of gravity with distance; an inverse square relationship. The rapid acceptance of Newton's theory as "law" and "universal" suggests that the scientific establishment were predisposed to think that way. We can draw parallels between the motion of a bird and a 'plane, but it does not mean they are propelled by the same motive force. The same can be said of apples and planets.

Two hundred years later, Einstein used a more complex 4-dimensional mathematical model to describe gravity as a distortion of space-time, but this was still only a way of describing gravity, not explaining it. Einstein was right in that the motion of the planets tells us something about space, but gravity cannot be defined as a distortion of something that has no separate existence. The search for the "god particle"; the Higgs Boson, was supposed to finally prove an actual gravitational mechanism. In 2012, having spent around $13 billion on the Large Hadron Collider, we were assured that the existence of the Higgs boson had been "statistically proven", but, as we are finding to our cost, commercial interests can distort research to the point where the results become meaningless, and there are very powerful commercial interests in a research project that has running costs of $1 billion per year.

The statistical "discovery" of the Higgs boson is really a complex and expensive way of convincing the scientific community that gravitation is still the "law", and still "universal", even though modern astronomers keep finding evidence to the contrary. The science media are still occasionally brave enough to ask the big questions, even if their conclusions are predictable. The front cover of *New Scientist* on 18/3/2017 read; "What's Up With Gravity? – The force that rules the universe makes no sense." On page 28, Mark Anderson wrote;

"To square the whirligig rotations of galaxies and galaxy clusters with our picture of gravity, we have to invent a whole new form of matter that no one has ever seen: dark matter. To explain why the universe's expansion is accelerating, we have to conjure up an equally mysterious essence known as dark energy. But what if we never really knew gravity at all? What if out there, beyond where we can easily keep an eye on it, the universal force doesn't stick to the rules?" [83]

In the same issue, Prof. Stacy McGaugh expressed his doubts about dark matter: "It's like God shouting: 'There's more to gravity, not more mass in the universe!'" [84] This is certainly a good starting point for re-examining gravity, but modern physicists are only willing to tweak Newtonian gravity, to venture to suggest that the inverse square law may not strictly apply when it falls below one 82 billionth of Earth's gravity, in accordance with Mordehai Milgrom's Modified Newtonian Dynamics (MOND).

In reality, Newtonian gravity is in need of a much more profound overhaul. In recent years, the Electric Universe Theory and Thunderbolts Project, founded by Wallace Thornhill and David Talbott, have made great strides in putting large scale electrical phenomena back into astronomy and cosmology. That these phenomena were ignored for so long is shocking enough, but there are profound implications for gravity's status as the universal glue. Thornhill suggests that gravity is a residual electromagnetic effect rather than a universal force, and he is not the first to suggest this. Newton's universal force may be no more than an approximation to gravitational acceleration near the Earth.

The Cavendish Experiment, performed in 1797 by Henry Cavendish, was the first experiment that appeared to confirm the universality of gravity by measuring an extremely weak force between two pairs of lead spheres, free to move on a torsion balance. Variations of the experiment continue to be used today, but Miles Mathis has shown, using modern understanding of radiation pressure, that the electromagnetic shielding caused by the lead spheres themselves could produce forces roughly 5 times greater than any gravitational attraction between the spheres[85]. This radiation pressure is similar to the tiny force produced on a mirror as it reflects sunlight – a phenomenon that could theoretically be exploited to propel light-weight space probes away from the Sun, using a lightsail. The Cavendish experiment did measure a tiny force between the suspended spheres, but we cannot assume that this was caused by gravitational attraction.

Earth's gravity certainly pulls all objects downwards, but it's a very big leap from this simple observation to the assumption that all objects must attract each other, as Newton supposed. Without Newton's Universal gravitation or Einstein's reformulation, modern cosmology rapidly starts to unravel. Rejecting the Newtonian model of gravity because of one imperfect experiment may seem unjustified, but variations of the Cavendish Experiment are still the only evidence we have of the apparent universality of gravity, and there is stronger evidence that our understanding of gravity really is fundamentally flawed.

Ralph Rene calculated the gravitational forces exerted by the Earth and the Sun on the Moon at new moon, when the Moon is positioned between the Earth and the Sun, and to his surprise, he found that the Sun should exert the *stronger* force. This means that the Moon should have been pulled out of its terrestrial orbit a very long time ago, and should be orbiting the Sun[86]. Proving this is straightforward. Even if we take the distance to the Moon when it is closest to the Earth (225,622 miles at perigee) and the distance to the Sun when furthest from the Earth (94.5 million miles at aphelion), and subtract one from the other to get the Moon-Sun distance, the ratio of the Earth-Moon distance to Moon-Sun distance is 1 : 417.8.

Newtonian gravity is inversely proportional to the square of the distance, so the Sun would need to be 417.8 squared times the mass of the Earth for the Earth and Sun to exert exactly the same pull on the Moon at new moon. $417.8^2$ is 174,500, but the Sun is estimated to weigh $1.99 \times 10^{30}$ Kg , which is 330,000 times the mass of the Earth, so the gravitational pull of the Sun on the Moon would be nearly twice the gravitational pull of the Earth on the Moon.

Defenders of Newtonian gravity try to dismiss Ralph Rene's argument by pointing out that the Sun attracts both the Earth and the Moon, but this is a spurious argument – we could also point out that the Earth should be exerting a force on the Sun, but that's not relevant either! The Earth can effectively be considered as stationary and the Sun-Earth pull ignored when considering the Moon. Newton's inverse square law does not hold true within the solar system, never mind the whole universe.

Rudolf Steiner suggested that we should really imagine the Earth and Sun spiralling around each other and following a lemniscate motion through space. For this to be true within the Newtonian model, the Earth and Sun would have to be of comparable mass, which would resolve Rene's lunar orbital problem, but would mean that the calculated masses of the other planets are also wrong. There is no easy way to prove or disprove this co-orbital model, but it would mean that star distances calculated by stellar parallax would have to be revised downwards as the diameter of the Earth's orbit would be substantially less than is currently assumed. In October 1920, Steiner explained that a complete understanding of the apparent motion of the Sun has still not been reached, and will only be reached when Copernicus' third law is properly understood:

"The interesting point in all this is that Copernicus was more advanced than we are today. We have simply omitted his third law from astronomy's post-Copernican development. Our astronomy has been developed without this third law, which states that other phenomena negate the yearly movements around the Sun that we calculate for the Earth. To do full justice to Copernicus, this law must be reintroduced." [87]

The Newtonian model of celestial mechanics and our preconceptions about electrons orbiting atomic nuclei are both built upon our everyday understanding of momentum. When we attach a ball to the end of a string and whirl it around, our hand has to exert a pulling force upon the ball to keep it in circular motion, and we assume that similar forces are needed to keep planets and electrons in orbit. But this outward projection of everyday observation into the stellar and subatomic scales may not be justified. At the macroscopic level, space and matter certainly appear to be independent, but, as quantum physics has shown, this distinction becomes blurred at the subatomic level.

Heisenberg's uncertainty principle states that a particle's position and *momentum* cannot be simultaneously defined. The bewildering implication of quantum physics is that, at the subatomic scale at least, space and matter may not be completely independent. But how can this be? A hundred years ago, quantum physics took us to the edge of a strange philosophical void, or was it actually a mirror? Either way, quantum physicists stepped back from the brink and remained within the traditional bounds of objectivity.

In projective geometry, all free motion is ultimately circular, even if it *appears* to be linear locally. The circular motion of planets and electrons may be a manifestation of the properties of the space in which they move, removing the need for gravity to hold planets in place, and the weak nuclear force to hold electrons in place. Newton's first law of motion may be the exception, not the rule, which means we should not presume to project our everyday experience of momentum onto atoms or planets.

To question the independence of space and matter now, in the face of all the amazing progress of modern science may seem like pointless retrospection, but this was one of the great philosophical questions to occupy Greek minds 2,500 years ago, and no completely satisfactory answer was ever reached. Parmenides rejected Leucippus and Democritus' atomic theory on the basis that atoms cannot move around in something that does not exist! If space, or the *void* as the Greeks called it, did not exist, then there would be no distance between the Earth and the Sun! After this promising start, however, Parmenides immediately lost his way and concluded, as nothing can come from nothing, that whatever exists has always existed and always will exist, therefore all change is an illusion. Rather than concluding that space must exist, he simply assumed that space does not exist because it does not *appear* to exist.

Democritus' theory that everything is composed of tiny atoms, so small that they "escape our senses" polarised the external world into indestructible, quantifiable matter and non-existent space, and science has, essentially, been built on the *assumption* that space is irrelevant in the study of Democritus'" solid, massy, hard, impenetrable, moveable particles".

This assumption went largely unquestioned until the early 19th century when the double-slit experiment began to undermine the solid, corpuscular model of matter. Electrons seemed to be turning into waves and then back into particles. As Keith Francis puts it;

"A particle is the exact opposite of a wave; a wave, whether its medium is water, air, or an electromagnetic field, spreads out in all directions from its point of origin until it happens to encounter an obstacle; it potentially occupies the whole ocean, the whole atmosphere or the whole of space." [88]

Schrodinger created his wave equation to try to model mathematically this ceaseless transformation of matter into space and back to matter, but if we imagine this constant dissolution and reformation of a particle as it moves, we may arrive at a new understanding of matter and space; an understanding that is closer to the spiritual view of matter as *maya* or illusion than the tiny billiard balls of reductionist science. A mobile particle, constantly dispersing into a wave and then "collapsing" and reappearing at a different point as a particle again, produces an *illusion* of motion similar to the *illusion* of motion on a cinema screen.

On a cinema screen, a moving train appears in one place, disappears completely and reappears in a slightly different position around 1/20th of a second later. Nothing has actually moved – it only appears to have moved. Obviously, the duration of each frame on a cinema screen depends entirely on the speed of the projector, whereas the duration (wavelength) of an atom is an inherent quality, dependent on its mass and the De Broglie equation. In the real world, 3-D atoms and trains have momentum, so real trains are a much more persuasive illusion!

Momentum, or more correctly inertia, is one of the defining qualities of matter, yet it turns out science still has no clear idea what matter, mass or inertia really are.

If inertia is defined as reluctance to move, then inertia/momentum can be thought of as a measure of a particle's embeddedness in time; a measure of its tardiness, its reluctance to turn, Schrodinger-style into a wave and back, rather than an ill-defined quality of matter itself. Suddenly there is nothing indestructible left of solid atoms – only 3-D illusions embedded in time – and space and matter only appear to be independent.

Quantum physics has challenged almost all the assumptions of classical physics but has not provided a coherent set of principles to replace classical physics. It has only thrown up awkward questions about the role of consciousness itself in the world around us, and even in physics experiments. Keith Francis writes:

"Consciousness is the central element in science because it is where the phenomena meet and interact. As the relativists and quantum physicists of the early twentieth century were to realise, the observer is part of the process. This realisation produced some pretty sensational new science and some apparently unanswerable questions but left the scientists' orientation to the natural world very much where it had been before." [89]

If wave/particle duality and entanglement seem incomprehensible in terms of classical physics, then the implications of Max Planck's *quantum of action* may be stranger still. If the convoluted space-time of matter only comes in discrete quanta, and is inseparable from the observer, doesn't that imply that consciousness itself must in some way be composed of discrete quanta? To continue the analogy of the train on a cinema screen, quantum physics is telling us that the screen, or space itself, is actually composed of tiny individual pixels like a computer screen.

Einstein himself was famously dismissive of the notion that the physical world might not be strictly deterministic; "I don't want to let myself be driven to a renunciation of strict causality before there has been a much stronger resistance to it . . . I can't bear the thought that an electron exposed to a ray should by its own free decision choose the moment and the direction in which it wants to jump away." [90]

Max Born took quantum physics to its logical conclusion - that atoms should really be thought of as arrays of numbers. Keith Francis elucidates;

"If we think of this in terms of an actual electron – a point particle in a geometrical orbit – we have the difficult task of trying to imagine the electron disappearing from one orbit and reappearing in another without having been anywhere in between. The relations between energy levels calculated from the lines in the hydrogen spectrum could best be depicted by rectangular charts rather than the equations of traditional algebra and calculus; or, in Born's slightly more formal language, "Heisenberg banished the picture of electron orbits with definite radii and periods of rotation because these quantities are not measurable. He demanded that the theory should be built up of quadratic (rectangular) arrays . . .""" [91]

From this idea, in 1925, Born, Heisenberg and Pascual Jordan formulated Matrix Mechanics which later became quantum mechanics. Born summed up the situation in his 1955 Nobel prize acceptance speech thus;

"So now we come to the final point – can we call something with which the concepts of position and motion cannot be associated in the usual way a thing, a particle? And if not, what is the reality that our theory has been invented to describe?" [92]

The successful application of Heisenberg's uncertainty principle and Schrodinger's wave equation has demonstrated the illusory nature of matter and motion at the atomic level, but the underlying discovery of quantum physics is even more shocking - atoms and even space itself are made of numbers, or more correctly; *arrays* of numbers or matrices. These arrays of numbers cannot be directly observed, but interact to create the *appearance* of space and matter.

# GEMATRIA AND THE CABALA

*In the beginning was the word,* and in the ancient Babylonian alphanumeric code of gematria, every word has a numerical equivalent. Whilst maths can accurately describe the behaviour of numbers in many ways, there will always be numerical problems that do not have perfect mathematical solutions – irrational numbers and the three- body problem[93] being just two examples. However accurate mathematical models may become, the real world always turns out to be more complex than it first appears. The Pythagoreans believed that "All is number", but that does not mean the entire universe can be reduced to the mathematical "unified theory of everything" that theoretical physicists so covet.

Numbers are, however, archetypically discrete and law-abiding, and as such, form the perfect basis for all causality, whether it be the mechanical causality of the material world or even the alchemical and spiritual causality of our conscious experience. If matter has slowly evolved out of consciousness, then the laws governing matter and consciousness must ultimately have some common basis or reflect each other. The old alchemists were onto something, and spiritual values such as *morality* may one day be applied to the external world as much as our internal world. To speak of the morality of the natural world seems strange now, but was still common in Goethe's time. Goethe still spoke of the "Deeds and sufferings of light", in contrast to Newton's lifeless corpuscular rays.

The ancient Cabala, or *Tree of Life* may seem an unlikely place to find insights into these subjects, but it can be thought of as an intuitive map of the internal geography of human consciousness itself. Just as modern psychology subdivides our thoughts, feelings and motives into conscious and subconscious, so the Cabalist's Tree of Life further subdivides our inner and outer life into 10 Sephiroth (singular Sephirah), symbolised by radiant "sapphires" with distinct archetypal psychological and spiritual characteristics. Why we don't normally perceive our own inner psychological and spiritual workings is a profound question, but we could equally ask why we are not normally aware of the workings of our own liver or kidneys. The answer is perhaps best expressed in the spiritual axiom that *You cannot perceive that which you are*, although according to spiritual science our consciousness is slowly evolving, and we will indeed learn to objectify and perceive all these inner processes over the coming millennia.

Rudolf Steiner would not have considered himself a Cabalist, but in 1922 he was able to confirm that the Sephiroth of the Cabala corresponded closely to his own deep insights into our inner and outer being;

"If we consider the whole human being as I have presented the subject in my *Theosophy,* in his nine parts, we find that from above down they are: spirit human being, life spirit, spirit self, spiritual soul, rational soul, sentient soul, sentient body, ether body and physical body. These are nine. They would not connect with earthly life in the right way if there were not also a synthesis, which is the tenth. This gives us ten, and these also appear in the Sephiroth of pre-Christian times." [94]

Though the Tree of Life certainly originated in pre-Christian times and has been closely associated with Judaism, the wisdom it contains is not exclusive to any particular religious denomination – the internal constitution of body, soul and spirit is the same everywhere on Earth. In a later lecture in 1924, Steiner further explained that the ten Sephiroth also correspond to Aristotle's ten categories, which became the starting point of Western philosophy, and science itself:

"This Tree of Life, this Tree of Sephirot, is the spiritual alphabet. More towards the West, in Greece, people also had a spiritual alphabet in ancient times. And in the time of Alexander the Great and Aristotle ten concepts were also given, but in a Greek form. You still find them listed today in all the schools of logic: existence, quality, state, and so on - again ten names, but different now because they are suited to the West. But people in the West understood these ten Greek letters of the spiritual alphabet just as little as the others just mentioned were understood. But look what an interesting story now takes place in humanity. Over in Asian those who still knew something had learnt to read the spiritual world through the Tree of Sephirot. And in the first centuries of Christianity those who still knew something of the spiritual world, over in Greece and Rome and so on, learnt to read according to the Aristotelian Tree of Life. But gradually all of them – those of the Tree of Sephirot and those of the Aristotelian Tree – forgot what these things were actually for, and could only list the ten concepts. And only now must we use these things again in such a way that we learn to read the spiritual world, otherwise gradually nothing will be known about the human being any more . . ." [95]

Irmgard Rossmann expands:

"It was understood in the philosophical history of Europe that Aristotle's categories contained the key to the secrets of the cosmos. The Aristotelian concepts encompass in the form of thought all the wisdom that could previously be experienced in the temple and mystery centres as instinctive knowledge and revelation. The ancient mysteries were already falling into decadence in Aristotle's time or were otherwise destroyed. It was the deed of Aristotle and his pupil Alexander the Great to spread this former mystery knowledge, now cast in the form of logical thought, throughout the culture of the known world. Western philosophy is founded directly on Aristotelian thought which came to Central Europe partly on direct paths from Greece via Rome, and partly by detour through the East, particularly through the cultural streams of Arabism and Judaism." [96]

The Tree of Life certainly can't be construed as anti-Christian either – the central Sephirah, called Tiphareth, is also known as the Christ-centre, and is latent within us all. In traditional Cabalism, these inner archetypal component parts evolve sequentially from some imperceptible spiritual source. They should, perhaps, be visualised as some kind of immaterial Russian dolls or spinning chakras rather than radiant sapphires, and they contain some surprising correlations with esoteric Christianity.

Heinrich Cornelius Agrippa (1486-1535) was a German physician, legal scholar, soldier and theologian, who also studied alchemy, gematria, the Cabala, and other subjects. Five hundred years after they were first published, his *Three Books of Occult Philosophy* may look hopelessly subjective, but they still contain a detailed exposition of the connection between two intriguing subjects; gematria and magic squares. Agrippa's books may have inspired Dr John Dee to produce his own Enochian magic squares a few decades later, though these do not appear to be true mathematical magic squares.

Though long revered in China, magic squares have generally been dismissed by western mathematicians as a pointless numerical game - a kind of medieval Sudoku - but they contain something that has been lost from almost all calculus and higher maths - they contain varying degrees of inner freedom. The five-square, containing just the numbers 1-25, can balance itself in over 200 million different ways, not including rotations and reflections, and larger squares contain exponentially higher levels of permutations. Even the mesmerising patterns of fractals do not contain this inner freedom, this inner life. Fractals are strictly deterministic - the spiralling patterns are completely predetermined by the mathematical algorithm from which they are generated.

The defining feature of our consciousness, wilfully ignored by modern science, is also freedom; the freedom to choose where to focus our attention, inwardly and outwardly at any time. If quantum physics is providing insights into the fabric of consciousness itself, as is claimed, then these quanta, or discrete numbers would need to be held within a framework that allows for varying degrees of inner freedom with varying levels of consciousness. Could Max Born's arrays of numbers that form the basis of matter and space, also form the basis of consciousness?

If matter and consciousness are the objective and subjective manifestations of Born's arrays of numbers or magic squares, this might begin to shed light on some of the oldest philosophical questions concerning the common origins of matter, space and consciousness. According to Theosophical cosmogenesis, our consciousness has developed through three pre-earthly stages in the distant past, called Old Saturn, Old Sun and Old Moon. At each of these stages, a denser form of matter and a greater degree of sentience evolved simultaneously, so warmth and awareness of time both appeared on Old Saturn, gaseous matter and awareness of one-dimensional space appeared during the Old Sun period, and liquid matter and our 2-D pictorial awareness evolved in the Old Moon period. Solid matter and our fully objective 3-D perception have only formed over the last hundred millennia or so, as our consciousness itself has become 3-dimensional (technically 4-dimensional if time is included as a dimension in the modern mathematical sense).

Steiner took this ancient knowledge several steps further. He pointed out that, in order to objectify a 2-D surface, we have to be able to stand in a third dimension, above those two dimensions, so to be objective about 3-D space, our thinking must already be four-dimensional, not including time. We are not yet conscious of this 4-D aspect of our own thinking, although this awareness will also develop in the future. One of these previous forms of space Steiner called *astral* space, which still exists around us. As early as 1909, Steiner was describing the spooky action-at-a-distance of quantum entanglement as a property of this astral space:

"As a circle becomes larger, the time needed to go around it grows longer. Ultimately, the circle becomes so huge that any given section seems almost like a straight line because there is so little difference between the circle's very slightly curved circumference and a straight line. On the physical plane, it is impossible to return from the other side as we would do on the astral plane. While the directions of space are straight in the physical world, space is curved in the astral world. When we enter the astral realm, we must deal with totally different spatial relationships." [97]

"Whenever I use geometric theorems, they turn into concepts at the borderline of normal conceptuality. Here, three-dimensional space returns us to our starting point. That is how in astral space, point A can work on point B without any connection between them." [98]

Astral space, as described by Steiner, differs from 3-D physical space in that complete objectivity is not possible within this strange type of space:

"Only one part of astral substance can be found outside, given to the subject in the environment. The other part must be added by subjective means, through personal activity. Conceptual and emotional forces allow us to extract the other aspect from what is given through active objectification. In the astral realm, therefore, we find subjective-objective substance." [99]

Ernst Marti suggests that light, which first appeared in the Old Sun period, still retains its one-dimensional quality even in our 3-D space, which is why light appears as one-dimensional *rays*, and liquid, which first appeared in the Old Moon period has retained its propensity to form 2-D planes. [100]

This is very different to the modern scientific assumption that all matter is composed of solid 3-D atoms that have existed since the dawn of time. It also means that the physical vestiges of these previous stages have to be attributed to other causes or marginalised as astronomical curiosities if we are to be kept within the modern material paradigm. The presence of cosmic background radiation and the decreasing solidity of planetary bodies with distance from the Earth, are just two physical reminders of this forgotten cosmological story.

If Mars is really as solid and rocky as the Earth and the Moon, then why do some meteorites create splash-like *lobate*[101] craters on the Martian surface? If these petal-shaped lobes are formed by partial melting of sub-surface ice by meteorite impacts, as NASA are keen to convince us, then why are there no lobate craters in the frozen Arctic tundra on Earth? Keeping us ignorant of the real significance of the vestiges of this astronomical alchemy is crucial to maintaining the reductionist paradigm around us, and it seems some people are willing to go to truly extraordinary lengths to preserve that paradigm, as we'll see in the last chapter of this book.

In Agrippa's time, magic squares were ascribed to the known planetary bodies, starting with Saturn (the 3-square), then Jupiter (the 4-square), Mars (5-square), the Sun (6-square), Venus (7-square), Mercury (8-square), and the Moon (9-square), and each of these also represented a different form of consciousness, or spirit. The unique feature of Agrippa's extant writings is that, using gematria, he calculated the numerical values of the names of these various spiritual beings and showed how they correspond to the numerical total of each line in the magic squares of the planets, demonstrating how different spirits; different forms of consciousness "fit into" different squares. The Sun square is composed of six lines (or columns), which correspond to the six Elohim from which the Sun was formed in biblical cosmogenesis.

In Agrippa's alchemical and magical works, the lines (or columns) of a magic square are driven by positive, creative forces, called the *Genius* or *Intelligences* of that square. So the six Elohim of the Sun square are the *Intelligences* of the Sun, each represented by the number 111, and the complete square is parasitized by its own destructive "Demon", called Sorat, with a corresponding value of 666, the total for the whole square.

On 12 September 1924, in one of a series of lectures about the Book of Revelation[102], Rudolf Steiner cleared up two millennia of speculation by confirming that 666 is indeed the number of Sorat, the "Sun Demon" rather than some nameless beast, and that knowledge of the "Intelligences and Demons" of all the planets was still being taught by the Catholic church up to the fifteenth century. In Hebrew, Sorat is spelt tau (400), resh (200), vau (6), samech (60), to be read from right to left. Steiner also drew the *sigil* of the Sun demon, which Donald Tyson has suggested is actually derived from the sequence of numbers within the Sun square[103].

If this was not extraordinary enough, Steiner then elaborated further. He explained that this malevolent force manifests through time in a 666-year cycle, first affecting events in the seventh century in Gondishapur, then bringing about the destruction of the Knights Templar in the fourteenth century. If Steiner was right, then some event of very long-term destructive influence at the very end of the twentieth century or start of the twenty first century was ultimately brought about by this being, acting through human vassals. The events of 9/11 certainly fit that description, but for the purposes of this book, the interesting implication is that various forms of consciousness do indeed manifest through magic squares, and that magic squares somehow unfold in a cyclic manner – they *are* consciousness embedded in time. Perhaps we should not be surprised at this – surely our normal consciousness can be characterised as the inner perception of change, which, of course requires the passage of time.

According to the Hermetic maxim *As Above, So Below*, man is a reflection of the whole universe. This makes no sense at all from the modern materialistic scientific viewpoint, which is based on the assumption that we are the accidental product of a random process of particle accretion, but it makes perfect sense if consciousness and matter have co-evolved. If all of the Sephiroth of the Cabala are contained within us, then all of Agrippa's Intelligences and Demons can influence us and potentially manifest through us. At this point, more striking parallels emerge between magic squares, the Cabala and Theosophy.

It's not possible to create a balanced 2x2 magic square. This suggests that 2-squares can never form matter, although they may underlie motion, in the same way that electrons are always in motion, but can never form matter on their own. The smallest balanced magic square is the 3-square, composed of the numbers 1 to 9 arranged in three rows and three columns, each adding up to 15. So the first balanced square to "come into existence" is the 3-square, and as such, this may mark the literal birth of the first time-cycle, though there would be no matter to perceive within this proto-space. In Theosophy, the first phase of pre-earthly evolution is referred to as the Old Saturn period, when there was no external matter, only something akin to our inner perception of warmth. Steiner confirmed that our perception of time began in the Old Saturn period,  one-dimensional space came into existence at the next (Old Sun) stage, two-dimensional space in the Old Moon stage, and three-dimensional space in our current stage of spiritual evolution[104].

The idea that magic squares somehow conjure time and space is startling indeed, but is actually the basis of maverick inventor John R R Searl's extraordinary work[105].

John Searl suffered severe hearing loss at an early age due to a head injury and in post-war Britain, his teachers assumed he was dumb rather than deaf. Consequently, he had to reach his own understanding of the world around him, which he duly did using magic squares and a sequence of dreams. By starting with progressively higher numbers, John Searl was able to create hundreds of magic squares for each size of square, and found that these squares "share" *timeframes* (determined by the lowest number in the square) and *spaceframes* (determined by the line total) in intriguing patterns reminiscent of the periodic table of the elements. Using this knowledge, he has been able to build devices that bend the "laws" of physics in more ways than one, but, like many genuinely original thinkers, he has been studiously ignored by academia.

In Searl's terminology, 15 is the *spaceframe* of the first 3-square, with subsequent *spaceframes* of 18, 21, 24 etc, and the *timeframe* of the first 3-square is 1. The first spaceframe shared by two squares is 42, which is the tenth level of the 3-square and the third level of the 4-square. Interesting patterns soon start to emerge – the 6-square (Sun square) can never exist in the same spaceframe as the 4-square or 8-square. The 6-square represents an inner Christian consciousness, and is always incompatible with the 4 and 8-squares, which suggests that these squares may represent profoundly anti-Christian forces which are, nonetheless, essential components of our psychological and even physical makeup. Traditionally, the presence of three crosses at Golgotha represents Christ holding *two* anti-Christian forces at bay; Lucifer *and* Ahriman/Satan.

In the Cabala, the first and second Sephiroth remain purely spiritual; they do not enter time and space. The first of the Sephiroth to manifest, to become perceivable, is not the first or second, but the third, called Binah, which is ruled by Saturn, Old Father Time himself, and in alchemy the 3-square is indeed ascribed to Saturn. Traditional Cabalists say that the correct understanding of the Tree of Life has long been hidden behind multiple layers of encryption to deter the unworthy. Is it possible that the Sephiroth of the original Tree of Life were magic squares?

The correspondence between the planetary "rulers" of the Sephiroth and the "rulers" of the magic squares continues through to the ninth Sephirah, Yesod, ruled by the Moon, but the really striking parallel is between the sixth Sephirah; Tiphareth, called the Christ-centre and the 6-square, or Sun square. As Steiner said in the same lecture on 12 September 1924;

"Let us consider that the Christian revelation as a whole is actually a Sun revelation, that Christ is the Being who comes from the Sun and who sends Michael with his hosts on ahead, just as Jehovah of old sent Michael on ahead. If we consider that we ourselves are now living in a Michael age we shall find that the Christ-impulse as a Sun Mystery appears very profoundly indeed before our soul."

Steiner explained elsewhere that the Christ - Spirit did not suddenly appear two thousand years ago, but has had a hand in guiding humanity since almost the dawn of time, behind the appearance of various Sun-Gods. The parallels between the 3-square (Saturn) and the third Sephirah - Binah, and between the 6-square (Sun) and the sixth Sephirah – Tiphareth, seem too strong to be coincidence. If we entertain the possibility that the Sephiroth of the original Tree of Life may have been magic squares, this would provide common causal ground for science *and* spirituality, matter *and* consciousness, which would ultimately put spirituality and the understanding of consciousness on the same rational footing as science.

Our thoughts and our souls may be conjured from the same stuff as atoms; that is, from numbers. This does not mean that modern science is in danger of returning to the subjective notions of the old alchemists, but rather that modern objectivity may ultimately be brought to bear on our own processes of perception. If matter and consciousness have co-evolved, then self –knowledge will one day be as concrete as our knowledge of the physical world.  This might also begin to explain Steiner's enigmatic words from the turn of the 20th century – in a lecture on 23 December 1904, he said;

"Before the end of the fifth epoch of culture, science will have reached the stage where man will be able to penetrate into the atom itself. When the similarity of substance between the thought and the atom is once comprehended, the way to get hold of the forces contained in the atom will soon be discovered and then nothing will be inaccessible to certain methods of working." [106]

This has rightly been interpreted as a prescient forewarning of the dangers of nuclear fission forty years before the development of nuclear weapons, but if matter and consciousness are reflections of each other, it could be argued that the atom has still more secrets to reveal. Steiner understood that the animal, plant and even mineral realms all represent previous stages of consciousness, so that even the lifeless mineral kingdom may support an extremely low form of consciousness, in line with traditional pantheistic spiritual teachings.

According to John Searl, magic squares can be subdivided into three main types, with different characteristics[107]. Type one are odd squares. However they are arranged, they tend to keep one number at their centre, which, according to Searl, gives them the capacity to rotate. Type two squares are those divisible by 4, which always have the same four numbers at their centre, giving them, in Searl's words, the capacity to "oscillate", and the remaining squares are type three, which can both rotate and oscillate, providing some kind of balance between type one and two. Considering the parallels between magic squares and the Tree of Life, it seems likely that these three types of square will manifest as fundamentally different types of consciousness, space and matter. If the 4 elements of physical matter manifest through odd squares, as seems likely, then our physical space is the only place where opposing spiritual forces can come into contact, working through type 2 and type 3 squares.

Modern science considers mathematical models of space with different dimensions and curvature, but space can be considered as a projection, an extension of our own consciousness. If we perceive the world around us in three dimensions of space and one of time, could it just be that those are the dimensions of our present state of consciousness? If consciousness has a numerical basis framed within magic squares, then the dimensions we perceive will depend on how many magic squares are "shared" at our particular level of consciousness, our particular *timeframe* and *spaceframe*. If the numbers within magic squares can be thought of as units (quanta) of space-time, then when we enter space-time, we should perceive space as a sphere surrounding us because, from the centre of a magic square, those units of space-time add up to the same value in every direction. Strictly speaking, this may only be true of type one (odd) squares as the even squares have no central number. Could this be the mythical "squaring of the circle", or more accurately, circling of the square upon entering the flow of time and causality?

In his book *Number, Time, Archetype*[108], Robert Dickter notes that there is a Pythagorean triplet of numbers at the centre of every odd magic square. Does this mean that the dimensions we perceive are only truly perpendicular at the centre of the space we occupy? This would lead to a truly anthropocentric relativity instead of Einstein's mathematical abstraction — finite but unbounded space would curve around us, wherever we choose to stand. Steiner was highly critical of Einstein's relativity, and emphasised many times the importance of not forgetting ourselves in our quest for knowledge:

"This will happen only when we progress to a form of natural science that truly includes the human being and observes phenomena within the human being. Taking these phenomena into account will allow us to develop a view of the events and processes of cosmic space. As Dr Unger also mentioned, the human being actually has been ousted from today's science, which disregards the human element. Ideas such as the theory of relativity, which certainly do not correspond to reality, are able to take hold only because modern science is so utterly estranged from reality that it deals with everything outside human beings but nothing that happens inside them. To think in ways that correspond to reality is a skill that humanity will have to relearn." [109]

If space is essentially nothing, as modern physicists believe, can there really be different types and shapes of nothing? Perhaps electric and magnetic fields should be thought of as different types of self-contained space rather than fields penetrating space. The alchemists certainly thought of the *spheres of the planets* as different types of space, but Steiner was the first to take this idea to its logical conclusion and introduce the concept of *counterspace*.

In our normal consciousness, we experience ourselves at the centre of the space around us — time, as it were, flows toward us from every direction, whereas, according to Steiner, in counterspace the opposite happens – we experience ourselves all around the periphery, looking inwards. This suggests that space and consciousness are not just inextricably linked - they are, in some circumstances, effectively the same thing. Counterspace is literally an unearthly type of consciousness as well as an unearthly type of space, and understanding counterspace is central to understanding the ether, or ethers, as Steiner explained in 1922:

". . . as soon as we move into the etheric realm, we need to apply an axial coordinate system that is the opposite – also qualitatively speaking – of the ordinary coordinate system. Ordinary theories about the ether of physics err in not taking this difference into account, making it difficult to define the ether. It is sometimes seen as a fluid and sometimes as a gas. It is wrong to apply a coordinate system that radiates from a central point to the ether. As soon as we enter the ether, we must take a sphere and construct the whole system from the outside in, instead of the other way round." [110]

Examples of phenomena that form from the outside inwards include tornadoes and whirlpools – slow circular motion at the periphery is gradually accelerated towards the centre by the Coriolis effect – a tornado cannot form from the centre outwards – there is almost no motion at the centre. Using ferromagnetic fluids, Ken Wheeler has been able to photograph magnetic fields, with extraordinary results – magnetic lines of force spiral inwards towards the North and South poles, without ever meeting, which means that magnetic fields also form from the periphery and have no centre.

Nick Thomas, in his book *Science Between Space and Counterspace*[111], posits that the speed of light is actually a scaling factor at the boundary of space and counterspace. Steiner was also rightly dismissive of the reductionist view of space as the insignificant medium of motion alone. As early as 1888, he had written;

"When we seek to discover what happens in that which is extended in space when the entities under consideration are being transmitted therein, we must conclude that it is always a motion. For a medium in which motion alone is possible must react to everything by way of motion, and all kinds of transmission which it must perform will be carried out by way of motion. When, therefore, I seek to discover the forms of this motion, I shall not learn what the thing is which is being transmitted, but only in what manner it is conveyed to me. It is sheer nonsense to say that heat and light are motion. Motion is merely the reaction of matter capable of motion to the action of light." [112]

Steiner assigned names to the three pre-earthly forms of space, or *ethers*: the warmth ether, light ether and chemical ether (sometimes called tone or number ether), but these are all still present around us alongside a fourth ether; the life ether. So we stand within at least four different forms of space, or ethers simultaneously, but complete 3-D objectivity is only found via our current Earthly physical senses. Guenther Wachsmuth examined the interaction of these 4 ethers in some detail in his 1932 publication; *The Etheric Formative Forces in Cosmos, Earth and Man*[113]. These ethers are the formative components of the external world, but are also reflected in our own inner alchemy.

Guenther Wachsmuth explained that these 4 ethers evolved sequentially over a cosmological timescale:

"In characterising the differences among the four kinds of ether we cannot restrict ourselves to the ascertained fact that they are distinguished in comparison with one another by the wave-lengths – that is, the degree of motion – which they call forth in the world of substance. Such merely quantitative distinctions of modern science do not at all suffice to explain the phenomena, qualitatively so utterly unlike, which the different kinds of ether produce in the world of substance. The relationship existing among the etheric formative forces is, rather, the following: The four etheric formative forces have proceeded phylogenetically one out of another, and proceed now ontogenetically one out of another; and, in reality, warmth ether has been metamorphosed – that is, has evolved into light ether; light ether into chemical ether; chemical ether into life ether. . . . The first two, warmth ether and light ether, have the tendency to expand, the impulse to radiate out from a given central point; they act centrifugally; whereas the other two, chemical ether and life ether, have the tendency to draw in toward a centre, the impulse to concentrate all in a given central point; their action is suctional, centripetal. This polarity of the two ether groups — the centrifugal, radiating, self-expanding will, and the suctional, centripetal will to draw inward, to concentrate — is an ultimate elemental principle lying at the bottom of all natural phenomena." [114]

After a lifetime of studying Steiner's work, however, Dr Ernst Marti concluded that Wachsmuth had not been consistent in his definitions of the elements, the ethers, and "formative forces" [115]. Marti believed that each element (fire, air, water or earth) manifests in physical space of differing dimensions, and that each corresponding ether manifests through counterspace of similar dimensions, so that new expansive, centrifugal and contractive, centripetal forces were created at each stage of our spiritual evolution.

This evolution of one form of space sequentially from another makes no sense at all in abstract mathematical terms — how can one dimension *evolve* from another if dimensions are simply independent mathematical variables? And how can space itself be expansive or contractive / suctional? But this does make perfect sense if these ethers represent the sequential evolution of magic squares, starting from the smallest 3-square, moving up through progressively higher timeframes to larger squares that share time and space in more complex multi-dimensional sets. This also fits the traditional Eastern understanding that the 4 elements and 4 ethers all evolved from an insubstantial *quintessence*.

Wachsmuth believed that these ethers ultimately have a threefold composition, in line with the Sephiroth of the Tree of Life, and he also correlated these with the spiritual structure of the inner Earth. In this model, the warmth ether would correspond to the first three Sephiroth of the Cabala (also known as Atziluth or the supernal triangle in the

Cabala), the light ether would correspond to the fourth, fifth and sixth Sephiroth (also known as Briah or the ethical triangle), the chemical ether to the seventh, eighth and ninth Sephiroth (also known as Yetzirah, or the astral triangle), and the life ether to the tenth Sephirah: Malkuth, the Earth.

In her book *The Mystical Qabalah*[116], Dion Fortune describes these triads of sephiroth as "Dimensions of consciousness". She elucidates further: "We shall be nearer an understanding of nature if we look for mind in the background than if we refuse to admit that the visible universe has an invisible framework. The ether of the physicists is closer akin to mind than to matter; time and space, as understood by the modern philosopher, are more like modes of consciousness than linear measures." These ideas have long been explored by cabalists. Kevin Townley's 1993 book *The Cube of Space*[117] examines them in detail, and considers the possible involvement of . . . magic squares.

Whether each evolutionary stage should correspond to two or *three* Sephiroth is an interesting question. We've already seen that the Sephiroth of the Cabala seem to fit the characteristics of magic squares, and in Patrice Chaplin's account of her initiatory journey through the Pyrenees in her book *The Portal*[118], her cabalistic guide let slip that the 12-square is also known as the New Jerusalem – a future state of consciousness.

The cabala is one of the few systems of thought that tries to encompass the subjective and the objective, the microcosm and the macrocosm, the spiritual and the physical, and provides useful insights in this regard. Macrocosm and microcosm are in some sense a reflection of each other. Dion Fortune puts it thus: "As we look at the Tree in the diagram we see Binah, Geburah and Hod upon the left side, and Chokmah, Chesed and Netzach upon the right side; this is the way we view the Tree when we are using it to represent the macrocosm. But when we are using it to represent the microcosm, that is our own being, we, as it were, back into it, so that the middle pillar equates with the spine, and the pillar that contains Binah, Geburah and Hod with the right side, and the pillar that contains Chokmah, Chesed and Netzach with the left side." [119]

If macrocosm and microcosm are reflections of each other, then the tenth Sephirah, Malkuth can be thought of as the plane of the mirror in which this reflection takes place – the objects we perceive are unique in that they simultaneously exist in the microcosm *and* the macrocosm. This is reflected in Wachsmuth's work as the macrocosmic ethers have their immanent internal equivalents. This reflection of macrocosm and microcosm is obviously not an actual spatial reflection, it is more of the nature of a *temporal* reflection. This means we may need to reintroduce another maligned and misunderstood concept into our thinking: Karma. Steiner was one of the very few who have had the courage to point out that this concept was an important part of early Christian teaching, and, contrary to popular opinion, is perfectly compatible with true Christianity. To grasp the totality of microcosm and macrososm in our minds, we would need to be able to stand outside time itself, as Goethe endeavoured to do two hundred years ago. So the Cabalistic/Masonic left/right spatial reflection should probably not be taken as a literal truth.

Aristotle himself used the term *ether* in a different sense, somewhat like a fifth element:

"It is that which is different from earth, water, air and fire. It is eternal and eternally revolves." [120] This may describe the first two Sephiroth, Kether and Chokmah, which are beyond time and space, like the Eastern *quintessence*. If we divide the rest of the Sephiroth into pairs, corresponding to the pairs of elements and ethers, then each new stage of evolution consists of one group 1 magic square – the physical manifestation of that stage of evolution, and one group 2 or 3 magic square – the formative or etheric aspect. This would explain how and why the elements and ethers evolve sequentially, one from another.

In this model, closer to Marti's than Wachsmuth's, the fire element would consist of just the 3-square and the warmth ether the 4-square.

The air element would be the 5-square and the light ether the 6-square, but the 4-square and 6-square can never "share" space, so the first division between light and dark, between space and matter would have naturally occurred in the Old Sun stage of evolution. Things become much more complex, however, if we then assume that the water element is the 7-square and the chemical/tone ether the 8-square, as the 8-square is never compatible with the 6-square, but can be compatible with the 4-square if constructed correctly. This suggests that the warmth and chemical/tone ethers would never have completely separated in the Old Moon stage of evolution, and that the light and life ethers may not separate entirely during our current stage of evolution on Earth

In Wachsmuth's understanding of the ethers, the warmth ether permeates the whole of the Earth, including the atmosphere, but is only really independent of matter in the upper reaches of the atmosphere, appropriately called the thermosphere. This may explain one of the strange contradictions of science – the temperature in the thermosphere can apparently reach $1,500^0$C, but there are so few gas molecules at this height that a thermometer would show an extremely low temperature. In the traditional understanding of the ethers, however, space itself, where permeated by the warmth ether can have a temperature – warmth is not simply atomic motion – it exists independently of more solid matter. This might also explain the Cosmic Microwave Background (CMB) that seems to come from every direction. It isn't the relic of a Big Bang, it's literally a region of warm space surrounding the Earth.

This would also explain why heat is such a problem for spacecraft, as the thermosphere extends about 500 Km from the Earth. If the warmth ether permeates this region, heat would not just be generated by the motion of a spacecraft – even a stationary spacecraft in the shadow of the Earth might overheat, even though conventional science says there would not be sufficient gas molecules to transfer any significant heat energy to the craft. The Apollo astronauts gave contradictory accounts about being too hot or too cold in cislunar space on their way to the Moon – no-one really knows if heat or cold would be the problem - if such a journey was ever undertaken.

There may be even stranger implications when considering the light ether. Wachsmuth believed that the light ether does not extend as far from the Earth as the warmth ether, but that implies that sunlight itself may only form below the thermosphere. In Wachsmuth's diagrams, the gasses of the upper atmosphere are continually replenished by life ether arriving from the Sun, but the life ether itself would not be visible. Obviously we can see the Sun when standing on the surface of the Earth, but can we assume that sunlight travels all the way from the Sun to the Earth in the form of "visible" light? This argument is further complicated by the fact that we do not directly perceive light at all, only the effects of light on matter.

If the military space pioneers of the '50s and early '60s had found that sunlight diminishes in intensity whenever we journey more than 500 Km from the Earth – a discovery that would have turned our assumptions about light and space upside-down - would they have decided it was in their national interest to announce those findings to the world, or to keep their enemies in ignorance? Just what astonishing truths did those world-leading German rocket scientists carry with them to America, Russia and Argentina at the end of World War 2? The symbolism of the black sun can be traced back to Tibetan Buddhism, a subject of great interest to the Ahnenerbe. Just what did they learn from the 120-volume *Kangyur,* obtained during their infamous 1938/9 expedition, and what was the real origin and purpose of the "Reich of the Black Sun"? [121]

The chemical/tone ether may also have qualities that run counter to the ill-defined modern conception of energy. The chemical ether is associated with the Moon and we tend to assume that moonlit winter nights are particularly cold because of the absence of cloud cover, when it may be that moonlight can actually cause cooling, particularly when the Moon is low in the sky, as the chemical/tone ether appears to act horizontally, as opposed to the life ether's vertical effect. Viktor Schauberger also believed that coldness is not simply the absence of warmth, and that heat and coldness are balanced at the anomaly point of water, $4^0$C. These ideas seem strange in comparison to the sweeping assumptions of modern science, but they are the keys to a much deeper science, a truly living science, predicated upon the old anthropocentric understanding of space: Up/down, left/right and forward/backward are not simply interchangeable variables – they are dimensions of our consciousness and have qualitative differences. Our horizontal perception is not quite the same as our vertical perception, and through body, soul and spirit we function in different types of space simultaneously.

# WALTER RUSSELL

Walter Russell (1871-1963) was another natural philosopher whose formal education ceased before the preconceptions of modern science were impressed upon his thinking. After a Damascene experience in 1921, when he was "aware of all things" and "able to perceive all motion", he started rationalising atomic physics and cosmology from a spiritual perspective. In Russell's cosmogony, atoms, planets and living things all start from a spiritual seed – an idea – which splits into two polar opposites upon entering the causal realm[122]. These polar opposites can exist for enormous periods of time, and can subdivide indefinitely, but must ultimately "void" or cancel each other – karma within the realms of mind *and* matter. During the growing, generative phase of all atoms, planets and organisms, centripetal and gravitational forces predominate over radiative, centrifugal forces and in the dissipative, dying phase centrifugal/radiative forces predominate, causing cooling, dissipation and death. Space itself gradually condenses into atoms, planets and living things, which then slowly dissipate back into space, though this process is not simply an on/off process, but a gradual change via a series of balanced intermediate stages between space and matter.

Russell's cosmogony is similar in many ways to the Theosophical view, but lacks Blavatsky and Steiner's grand historical perspective on the *evolution* of human and lower forms of consciousness over aeons of time. But Russell was still able to shine a very illuminating light on the shortcomings of modern science. According to Russell, thought waves are reproduced throughout the universe at 186,000 miles/second. Coulomb's law is wrong – opposites do *not* attract, though they sometimes appear to attract. Coldness is not simply the absence of heat, but should be considered independently of heat. The cold in the great expanse of space perfectly balances the "heat in all the suns of the universe". Gravitation is the process by which space condenses into matter, which means matter should gain *inertia, not just mass* as it falls, and Newton's inverse square law is just an *effect, a consequence* of this process.

According to Russell, cause and effect are part of nature's "cinema motion picture"; Space condenses into matter via the North and South poles of the Sun, which then radiates heat through its equatorial plane; Newton's laws of motion are just hypothetical and do not actually correspond to the real world; Planets *accelerate* towards their perihelion, even though there is no mass there to attract them; Matter neither attracts nor repels matter, it simply seeks balance with its environment, and that balance point will gradually change; Kepler's first law needs to include four poles or foci rather than two to accurately model planetary motion; When subatomic particles stop moving, they cease to exist, and there are 9 octaves of chemical elements, that develop sequentially from the inert gasses over a long timescale, with carbon the only perfectly solid cubic element.

John Searl's understanding of magic squares creates a cycle of octaves of increasing complexity, very similar to Russell's periodic spiral of the elements. The Walter-Russell.com website has some interesting articles that explore the consequences of Russell's "New concept of the universe". One article, called Funny Bones (20/12/17) considers the implications for astronauts and spacecraft that might travel through space for long periods. According to Russell, in the reduced gravity of space, astronauts and their craft would have to reach a new equilibrium between expansive and contractive forces – they would actually radiate physical mass until they reached a density commensurate with their distance from the Earth. The problem of bone loss in space is well known, but Walter Russell may have been the only one to truly understand the cause, at least 30 years before the space race had even begun.

As with all the other problems of space travel, NASA now seem to be brushing the problem aside with just a few reassurances about the benefits of regular exercise regimes for astronauts. After 192 days on the Space Station during which she apparently suffered no bone loss, Sunita Williams claimed that her bones must have gained external mass at exactly the same rate that they lost internal mass[123]. But she showed absolutely no signs of the disfiguring effects of gaining external bone mass. How can that be? Leaving Williams' reassurances aside, the real implications for our dreams of space travel are catastrophic. The radiation detected in the Van Allen belts may be a symptom of this reciprocal relationship between space and matter – the danger may be within, not without, which would mean that no amount of shielding would protect us from the Van Allen belts.

This also fits quite well with the Theosophical and Anthroposophical view – truly solid matter only exists on the Earth and the Moon. When we pass beyond the limits of the life ether, however this ether is defined, matter must start reverting to its previous liquid state, and when we pass beyond the limits of the chemical ether, matter must slowly revert to the gaseous state. Four- dimensional matter cannot exist in three-dimensional space. Rockets will never take us to other planets, although there may ultimately be some way around this problem using much more advanced technology that can somehow generate space or the ethers as it travels. Whether this kind of technology can ever be developed using Blavatsky's, Russell's, Schauberger's and Tesla's universal principles, is an interesting question – if it hasn't already fallen into the wrong hands.

# THE MARS ROVERS

If the Apollo missions were really a conjuring trick to keep us from the path of collective self-discovery; to keep us in thrall to the military-industrial-computing complex, then some of the other achievements of NASA and the other space agencies must also be illusory. Exactly where reality ends and illusion begins is not clear – there are even suggestions that Augmented Virtual Reality software and other trickery is already being used to add floating 3-D objects into videos of the International Space Station in real time. This is now possible - the astronauts would have to wear special Augmented VR contact lenses that relay an image of the VR objects into their eyes so they can "see" the virtual objects around them. The latest computer gaming technology may have some unexpected applications! This does not mean that the Space Station itself does not exist – it is certainly visible from terrestrial telescopes – but life may be considerably more difficult up there than NASA, Roscosmos, JAXA, CSA and the ESA would care to admit.

The pictures from all the space probes that have explored the solar system may be genuine – it would be impossible to verify them using terrestrial telescopes anyway. According to Walter Russell, all solid matter must start to lose its density and mass as it leaves the Earth, but he gives no timescale for this process - the densest metals might possibly last for years, so the data and images from interplanetary probes may be genuine.

The contrast between fact and fiction is more evident when we look at Mars, however. Steiner understood that, upon reaching Mars, we have left the solid, rocky planets behind and we are, at best, on a semi-solid surface. This fits well with the evidence from terrestrial telescopes – Mars' distinctive lobate craters and rampart craters are exactly what we should expect to see on such a semi-solid surface[124]. But, starting with the Viking landers in 1976, through the 2004 Spirit and Opportunity Rovers and the 2012 Curiosity Rover, NASA have supplied us with a completely different picture of Mars - a dry, rocky surface reminiscent of many desert areas on Earth. As with the Apollo missions, the only way to assess the veracity of NASA's claims is to look at the evidence very closely, and once again, there's something devilish lurking in the detail.

From 1964 to '71, Mariners 4,6,7 and 9 photographed the Martian surface, then on 20th July 1976, Viking 1 landed on the surface, and was almost immediately caught up in controversy. NASA maintain that they have to digitally alter the colour balance in their images from Mars in order to compensate for the pinkish-brown hue of the dusty atmosphere. The very first colour image from the surface of "Mars" (PIA 00563) was of beautiful blue sky over a brown rock-strewn surface – a picture that could have come from a thousand different places on Earth[125]. NASA then quickly removed this image and replaced it with the "correct" version, showing a reddish surface and pink sky, and have never satisfactorily explained this "error". If they were compensating for the pinkish incident light, then the first image should have been the "correct" one – so why was it replaced with a more "Mars-like" one?

At the first Viking press conference, Carl Sagan deflected questions by saying that "...it was done before the appropriate colour calibration chart data had been incorporated." [126] Are we really to believe that the Martian sky is blue when you forget to compensate for the pink light? Surely it should be the other way around! Years later, Holger Isenberg[127] reconstructed some of the Viking 1 images using NASA's own filter response data, and found . . . pale blue skies! This whole argument then resurfaced in 2004, when it could clearly be seen that the colours of the calibration target on the Spirit Rover were completely wrong in NASA's images. Incident pink light can turn a white surface pink, but on the calibration target, blue was apparently turning pink on Mars, which is not possible - it should have just appeared darker blue. Since those first Viking images, conspiracy theorists have leapt to the conclusion that NASA are hiding the blue skies of Mars, when there is a much more prosaic, if disturbing explanation – the images are not coming from Mars at all. NASA now present all their images as "false colour images" and leave us to guess what they may or may not be hiding.

The stated mission of the Viking Landers was to search for signs of life on Mars. The Pyrolytic Release experiment, the Gas Exchange experiment and the Gas Chromatograph/Mass Spectrometer all failed to find signs of organic compounds. The Labelled Release experiment generated much excitement when a positive result was detected, but NASA decided this was probably a false reading caused by perchlorates in the Martian soil. The interesting thing about this drama was that this ambiguity would have been avoided if NASA had used Wolf Vishniac's "Wolftrap" labelled release apparatus on the Viking landers, as was originally planned. Vishniac's equipment would have not have given a false-positive reaction to perchlorates, and yet was replaced as a "cost-saving" exercise even though the total cost of the Viking programme was over a billion dollars. It's almost as if they wanted an ambiguous result from at least one of the experiments, just to generate some excitement and interest.

Wolf Vishniac himself was found dead at the foot of a cliff in the Asgard Range in the Dry Valleys of Antarctica two years before the first pictures came back from the Viking landers. Some of the more remote areas in the McMurdo Dry Valleys, such as the ancient boulder-strewn Sirius Area of Mount Feather and the unexplored Friedman Valley are really strikingly similar to the Viking lander photos – another interesting coincidence.

Once the Viking 1 lander had stopped transmitting in 1982, there were no further images of the Martian surface until the Pathfinder Lander delivered the 11Kg Sojourner Rover to the Ares Vallis region in July 1997, and transmitted images of another rock-strewn plain. This was followed in January 2004 by the much larger solar powered identical twin Spirit and Opportunity Rovers, each weighing 185 Kg. The Spirit Rover landed $14^0$ South of the Martian equator in Gusev crater and covered 7,730m before getting stuck in sand in December 2009, having lasted 20 times longer than its planned 90-day mission. The Opportunity Rover landed $2^0$ South of the equator on the other side of Mars and was still transmitting in 2018. We are told this rover has travelled over 45 Km on the Martian surface and has lasted over 50 times longer than its planned mission.

The longevity of Spirit and Opportunity is mainly attributed to miraculous periodical "cleaning events" [128] caused by dust devils on the Martian surface. NASA claims these dust devils remove the dust from the rovers' solar panels, boosting the efficiency of the panels by up to 50% each time, allowing the rovers to keep recharging their batteries. Leaving aside the obvious questionability of these "optimised" batteries lasting over 14 years of continuous recharging on Mars, this is about as likely as your car being periodically cleaned by dust devils in an arid area of the Earth. The improbability of this explanation was compounded by the fact that NASA have no photographic evidence of this process as it only seems to happen at night. Dust devils are caused as warm air rises, heated by the warm surface in hot sunlight. Just how much nocturnal sunlight is there on Mars to generate these industrious somnambulant Martian dust devils?

The Spirit rover got off to an uncontroversial start on another rock-strewn plain, but only 34 Martian days (sols) into its mission, the Opportunity rover became mired in an under-reported controversy that briefly exposed the true mentality of NASA's Rover mission controllers to the whole world. Moving in to investigate a rock called El Capitan only yards from its landing site, the rover's microscopic imager provided a beautiful photo of a fossilised ringed stem a few cms long, topped by a branched crown. Richard Hoover, NASA employee for over 40 years and founder of the Astrobiology Research Group at the NASA/Marshall Space Flight Center immediately recognised it as a Crinoid fossil, only to find that this, NASA's most important discovery in half a century of space exploration, had been deliberately ground to dust only three and a half hours after its discovery! [129]

On asking NASA astrobiologist David McKay to explain this asinine destruction, Hoover was told that it was done to "look at the inside, looking for carbon". Hoover had a problem accepting this answer, however, as he puts it:

"Anyone who does much in the field of palaeontology knows that you don't have to find carbon to find fossil . . . You would never have a palaeontologist say "Gee. That may represent a new genus of life on Earth. Where's my rock hammer? I want to smash that to bits."" [130] Hoover, like others before him, then assumed that NASA are hiding evidence of life on Mars. But crinoids are a species of echinoderm that has evolved on Earth - surely Ockham's razor dictates that the simpler explanation is the true one. A handful of individuals are not hiding the existence of life on Mars – why would they? – NASA's budget would double overnight if they found proof of life on Mars. In reality, whenever the NASA rovers find evidence of life, it is studiously ignored or, in this instance, ground to dust because a handful of individuals know that any evidence the rovers find will lead to a much more disturbing discovery.

The Spirit rover provided the next controversy by photographing something indistinguishable from lichen on a rock surface on sol 386 of its mission[131]. NASA dismissed this as a dust pattern left on the surface by the rover's Mossbauer spectrometer, but the distinctive Maltese cross shape of the Mossbauer was captured in an Opportunity Rover photo in 2014 and looked nothing like the foliose pattern on the rock[132]. In 2013, on sol 3540, the Opportunity rover created more controversy when a small piece of dry fungus-like material appeared next to the rover. NASA decided this was a rock dislodged by one of the rover's own wheels and named it Pinnacle Island, even though it really did not resemble a rock. Rhawn Joseph has rightly concluded that Pinnacle Island was very probably a piece of Apothecium[133] – a fungal/bacterial mat. NASA spent four weeks "investigating" Pinnacle Island, but provided very few close-up photos to support their supposition that it was just an inert piece of rock.

The really unique feature of the Opportunity rover's travels was the discovery of small 3-5mm iron oxide (haematite) spherules, called Martian Blueberries, apparently littering large areas of the Martian surface and embedded in Martian rocks. They were dubbed *blueberries* on account of their blue appearance in NASA's images, but this leads us, once again to question the colour in the images. The Martian atmosphere is less than 1% of the Earth's, and 95.3% of that very thin air is Carbon dioxide and only 1.6% Oxygen, so iron should oxidise, if much more slowly than on Earth. So these haematite spherules should have much the same colouration as on Earth – a wide range of colours from black to grey and brown to red, but not blue. NASA have never offered any explanation why these spherules appear *blue* in their images.

Most of the embedded spherules in the Opportunity images are found within a soft *evaporitic matrix*. This fits the belief that the spherules have slowly formed over millennia as salt water has dried out. But this same process of evaporation also takes place on Earth, leaving a perfectly flat, layered "matrix" called a salt-flat, a phrase NASA's rover directors seem strangely averse to using. According to the official timeline, the Opportunity rover spent the first seven years of its mission crossing just such a salt-flat on Mars, photographing around 50 craters along the way before reaching the mountainous rim of Endeavour crater. The majority of that salt-flat was covered in long dark sand-dunes, or was it volcanic ash? – another association NASA are keen to avoid. This landscape may not have been quite as unearthly as NASA would have us believe.

The embarrassing photos continued when the Phoenix Lander arrived to search for signs of life in Northern Martian latitudes in 2008. Once again, NASA had nothing much to report, but American space enthusiast Ron Bennett decided to put a series of microscopic images from the lander into a short animation to look for signs of movement in the Martian soil, and found much more than he expected. Small blurry pink and brown objects, roughly the size of a grain of sand were quite clearly moving, if only slowly in the cold soil sample[134]. Once again, a damning piece of evidence was wasted as Bennett concluded that the tiny mobile lifeforms could only be tardigrades (microscopic maggot-like creatures) as only tardigrades could possibly survive the hostile Martian conditions. Even though Bennett misidentified this soil fauna because of his own preconceptions, it should have been seized upon by NASA as proof of Martian life, but instead Bennett was steadfastly ignored.

Once again, the silence from NASA was deafening. In fact, any acarologist would immediately recognise this soil fauna as soil mites. They look like blurry blobs under a light microscope because their legs are thin and translucent – their legs only really show up under an electron microscope, which certainly wasn't part of the equipment on the Phoenix lander. According to NASA, the Phoenix lander was buried under solid carbon dioxide snow due to its proximity to the Martian North pole, but they failed to provide any photos or data from the lander to substantiate this totally unique event, completely new to science[135].

In 2014, Richard D Hall brought his considerable engineering experience and documentary skills to the subject of NASA's sleight of hand, not long after the 899 Kg nuclear-powered Mars Science Laboratory Curiosity Rover landed on Mars, and he has tried, using FOIA requests, to get some answers from NASA, which have not been forthcoming. Richard tried to obtain some evidence, any evidence that any of the Mars rovers had been through industry-standard testing, or that any of the complex sky-crane landing mechanism had been tested and proven on Earth, but was rewarded with . . .nothing.[136]

Perhaps the first question we should all be asking about the Curiosity Rover is how a 4 tonne vehicle (rover + sky crane + heatshield) was slowed from an entry speed of 13,000 mph to 900 mph by a heatshield in an extremely thin atmosphere. Mechanical engineer Fred Seddon calculated that even if this were possible, the specific heat capacity of the Phenolic Impregnated Carbon Ablator allegedly used in the heatshield would have to be hundreds of times greater than any known material. Seddon accordingly christened it *Amazium or Thermalinfinitium*[137] – another miraculous but strangely ill-defined invention to add to NASA's growing catalogue. It's also doubtful that a parachute would even deploy in the thin Martian air to further slow the rover's descent. The Martian surface pressure of only 600 pascals is equivalent to the pressure at over 100,000 ft above the Earth's surface. Parachutes do not normally deploy at this altitude – they don't inflate, they simply spin around and become unusable.

This absence of verifiable science behind the rover programmes was most clearly on display at the landing briefing after Curiosity landed in 2012, when Adam Steltzner, lead engineer for Curiosity was unable to answer the simplest questions from journalists about the rover[138]. The whole briefing had the air of a slick PR production rather than the gravity of a great scientific achievement. Obviously this doesn't prove anything, but is symptomatic of NASA's increasing preoccupation with presentation rather than substance.

The images from Curiosity have also sparked plenty of controversy. When corrected for NASA's usual dusty pink hue, the hills around Mt Sharp have exactly the layered quality of a high definition 3-D computer landscape. Real landscapes features can be incorporated and rearranged within a 3-D computer database by using LIDAR (Light Detection And Ranging). LIDAR or LADAR is the laser equivalent of Radar. With a powerful laser and fast processor, there is almost no limit to how much real 3-D geological detail can be added to a CGI-enhanced landscape[139]. This can then be combined with high-definition photography to create whole new worlds, from which individual "photos" can be generated by digitally adding the distortion created by real photographic lenses. Using this technology, a rover could drive up to a real rock somewhere on Earth and do every kind of analysis, all within a suitably "Martian" landscape, without ever leaving the Earth.

For such a trick to work, NASA would need to use the most remote and barren locations on the Earth, and cold desert regions would fit the Martian narrative better than hot ones. But life, or at least fossilised life, has a habit of showing up even in the most remote desert areas, and would be extremely difficult to eliminate from the background in high definition landscape photos.

On only the 52nd sol of Curiosity's adventure, in a series of high-definition landscape images, the Curiosity Pancam caught what appears to be a small rodent – clearly visible in at least three images[140]. There are, of course, hundreds of Youtube videos of NASA images that look like birds, aeroplanes, submarines and nightmarish aliens, but a rough calculation of scale usually shows them to be what they are: pareidolia – an over-active imagination. But there are several features that distinguish the little rodent from all this background "noise". One is that Curiosity photographed the same area from the opposite direction three weeks later, on sol 77, and the small "rodent-like rock" had completely disappeared[141]. The second is that, using NASA's own data about the exact location of the rover at the moment of each photograph, the position of the rodent can be triangulated, so its size can be accurately determined at 12-13 cm[142]. So the perfectly lemming-like "rock" is exactly the same size as a collared lemming and seems to have the power of independent movement. Collared lemmings are found throughout the Canadian Arctic, including Haughton Crater on Devon Island, where NASA test their Mars Rovers. Should this really be dismissed as pareidolia, given what we already know about NASA?

Despite all the evidence, the possibility of a deception of this scale is usually dismissed on the grounds that hundreds, or possibly thousands of NASA and ESA employees would be involved, so it would not remain secret very long. But Richard D Hall uncovered very good evidence that there are choke-points in the flow of data from NASA that can be used, and are being used to keep even the majority of NASA personnel completely in the dark about the real source of NASA's images.

Soon after landing in 2004, the Spirit rover developed a software glitch which was investigated by two independent software engineers who decided to publish their discoveries (anonymously) on the AstroEngineer's Blog[143] in 2010. Richard summarises their account[144]:

"While investigating a software failure on the Spirit rover, one of the engineers decided to download from the rover a memory dump of large sections of the rover's computer code. He compared the computer code with a version he thought the rover should have been running and found some differences. He investigated the functionality of the additional computer code which seemed to have been added to the Spirit rover. After much investigation of this additional code, he and another engineer came to the conclusion that the rover was interfaced to an additional undisclosed piece of hardware, and was communicating with this mystery hardware. They decided that the hardware was probably a radio communication device of some sort with very low power consumption. The additional computer code also contained image manipulation functions which had the capability to manage, modify and delete images from Spirit's memory. None of this functionality should have been present in the code. In order to find who had added the mystery computer code, one of the engineers executed some of the functions on their own Earth-based computer platform, and then compared the resulting files for similarities with files from the JPL computer network. They were able to trace a user who had deleted files which had been generated using the same mystery software they had downloaded from the rover. The department where the computer was located was "Quantum Sciences and Technology". They later identified a protocol the user was running to communicate with the Spirit rover via a data server with the undisclosed interface and wrote some software to eavesdrop on the protocol. The eavesdropping revealed that somebody within Quantum Sciences and Technology was accessing data from the rover almost in real time. This seemed impossible because it takes signals approximately 20 minutes before they arrive at the Earth. The engineers surmised the reason why this was possible, was because a technique had been developed by Quantum Sciences and Technology for faster than light communication between Earth and Mars."

Of course, as Richard points out, the only plausible explanation for someone being able to access and edit the Spirit rover images in real time, before being transmitted "to Earth" is that the rover is, actually, still somewhere on the Earth. The rover images are edited before anyone at NASA or JPL even sees them. Creating the illusion that the rover data has been received from Mars via the Deep Space Network would then only involve a very small number of personnel.

Is this all just a conspiracy theory? No – it's more than that. It's evidence of a long-term malevolent influence on independent thought itself, although a few individuals are obviously aware of the real nature of this game, and are willing participants. In our haste to embrace the scientific view, we have turned our backs on something that thrives in the penumbra of lazy supposition, something that ultimately wishes to limit and control human free will itself. On the positive side, the very existence of such a monstrous distortion of the truth is evidence enough that humanity really has been endowed with the greatest spiritual gift of all – Free Will.

We are all jurors in the court of public opinion and must always return to the evidential trail to have any chance of reaching the truth. In the words of Dr Judy Wood:

"If you listen to the evidence carefully enough, it will speak to you and tell you exactly what happened. If you don't know what happened, keep listening until you do. The evidence always tells the truth. The key is not to allow yourself to be distracted away from seeing what the evidence is telling you." [145]

# REFERENCES

1. Buzz Aldrin to Neil Armstrong on first seeing the Apollo footage, whilst in quarantine.
2. Ralph Rene, Chapter 6 of *NASA Mooned America,* available as a pdf.
3. Gerhard Wisnewski, *One Small Step?* , Clairview books, p90
4. Exopolitics.org, *Did Armstrong and Aldrin receive death threats to keep Moon secrets?*
5. Ralph Rene, preface to *NASA Mooned America*
6. James DeMeo, orgonelab.org/miller.htm
7. James DeMeo, orgonelab.org/miller.htm
8. James DeMeo, orgonelab.org/miller.htm
9. Bennett and Percy, *Dark Moon,* Aulis Publishers, p128
10. Jayweidner.com, Kubrick's Odyssey
11. Checktheevidence.com, or Youtube: Richard D Hall Andrew Johnson Apollo Conspiracy.
12. Aulis.com/stereoparallax.htm, or search: Oleg Oleynik.
13. This quote has been widely attributed to Twain, though its exact origin is unknown.
14. En.wikipedia.org/wiki/Stolen_and_missing_moon_rocks.
15. AMLAMP records are available to download. Work continues under aegis of ANSMET
16. Lunar and Planetary Science XXXII (2001), "Lunar Meteorite Source Crater Size: Constraints from Impact Simulations". J N Head.
17. Moonfaker.com, Youtube channel: Youtube.com/user/WhiteJarrah
18. Jarrah White Youtube channel, Moonfaker Radioactive Anomaly, parts 1-23
19. *Journey to Tranquility*, Young, Silcock and Dunn, 1963
20. Telegraph.co.uk (22/5/2009), Sir-Bernard-Lovell-claims-Russians-tried-to-kill-him-with-radiation.
21. Americanmoon.org/VanAllen/letters/index.htm
22. Reuters.com/article/us-space-radiation/whats-keeping-us-from-mars-space-rays-say-experts

23. Jarrah White Youtube channel, Moonfaker Radioactive Anomaly videos, or Rene, *NASA Mooned America,* Chapter 15.
24. Jarrah White, Moonfaker videos 12-14
25. Chris Kraft, Popular Mechanics 2009. Quoted by Phil Kouts in Nexus Magazine June-July 2016, "Towards a Moon Base – Leaving Apollo's legacy behind" p49.
26. Aulis.com/censored.htm
27. Phil Kouts, Nexus Magazine Aug-Sept 2014, "Is There Any Hope for a Moon Base?" p35
28. NASA's Exploration Systems Architecture Study – Final Report (NASA-TM-214062) 2005, p629. Kouts, Nexus Mag. Aug-Sept 2014, "Is There Any Hope for a Moon Base?"
29. Government Accountability Office, "NASA: Ares 1 and Orion Project Risk and Key Indicators to Measure Progress" (GAO-08-1861) 2008, p14.
30. Government Accountability Office, "NASA: Constellation Program Cost and Schedule Will Remain Uncertain Until a Sound Business Case is Established" (GAO-09-844) 2009, p11.
31. GAO 2008, p10. Phil Kouts, Nexus Mag. Aug-Sept 2014, p72
32. Phil Kouts, Nexus Mag. June-July 2016, "Towards a Moon Base – Leaving Apollo's Legacy Behind.", p52
33. Youtube: "Sending a laser to the Moon – Horizon – Explore BBC".
34. New York Times, 5/11/1963, "Soviet Bounces Light Beam off Moon in a Laser Test." Quoted by Jarrah White in Youtube video: Moonfaker: Exhibit D, part 6.
35. BBC News (30/7/2012), "Apollo Moon Flags Still standing, Images Show."
36. Jarrah White, Youtube video: Moonfaker: LRO, Flag or no Flag?
37. Richard Hoagland and Mike Bara, *Dark Mission*, p81-82
38. Nasa.gov/directorates/heo/library/reports/lunar-artifacts.htm
39. Wisnewski, *One Small Step,* p15, from United Soft Media Verlag GmbH: Mission Mond DVD
40. Wisnewski, *One Small Step,* p20, from English Pravda, 12/4/2001
41. Wisnewski, *One Small Step,* p14.

42. Wisnewski, *One Small Step,* p12, from lostcosmonauts.com: The First Woman in Space.

43. Wisnewski, *One Small Step*, p31.

44. Wisnewski, *One Small Step,* p41-43.

45. http://www.dailymail.co.uk/news/article-2342265/Yuri-Gagarins-mysterious-death-finally-solved.html

46. Ralph Rene, *NASA Mooned America*, preface.

47. Wisnewski, *One Small Step,* p21-23

48. Istvan Nemere, *Gagarin- A Cosmic Lie.* Not translated from Hungarian.

49. Elliot Haimoff, *The Cosmonaut Coverup.* Global Science Productions, 1999.

50. David Percy, *What Happened on the Moon?* Video, part 2 , *Aulis.com*

51. "Jock" Bruce Gardyne, writer for FT and Telegraph said so at the time: *Was Gagarin Russia's answer to Piltdown Man?*, Daily Telegraph, 21/4/1986.

52. *Are these failings of Western science deliberate or accidental?* Aether, The Transcript, Pathway Initiatives 2006, p162.

53. Joseph P Farrell, *The Philosopher's Stone,* Feral House, 2009.

54. Nick Cook, *The Hunt for Zero Point,* Century, 2001.

55. Richard C Hoagland and Mike Bara, *Dark Mission, The Secret History of NASA,* Feral House, 2007, p278.

56. Rense.com, *Astronaut Reveals NASA Mind Control Program Involving Kids.*

57. Peter Hyatt and Richard D Hall, Youtube: *Analysing The Astronauts,* parts 1-3. Reproduced with Richard D Hall's permission.

58. Joseph Farrell, *Reich of the Black Sun – Nazi Secret Weapons and the Cold War Allied Legend,* Adventures Unlimited Press, 2004.

59. http://www.dailymail.co.uk/news/article-4252164/Files-suggest-Nazis-tested-NUCLEAR-BOMB-WW2-ended.html.

60. Joseph P Farrell, *Secrets of the Unified Field,* Adventures Unlimited Press, Chapter 2.

61. Joseph P Farrell, *Secrets of the Unified Field,* Adventures Unlimited Press, p38.

62. https://en.wikipedia.org/wiki/Eisenhower%27s_farewell_address
63. Rupert Sheldrake, *The Science Delusion,* p16.
64. Rupert Sheldrake, quoting Terence McKenna, *The Science Delusion,* p65.
65. Dr Edi Bilimoria, *Aether – The Transcript,* p101.
66. Rupert Sheldrake, *The Science Delusion,* Coronet, 2012.
67. Rupert Sheldrake, *The Science Delusion,* p90-91.
68. Rupert Sheldrake, *The Science Delusion,* p92.
69. Scientific American, Feb 2017, *Pop Goes the Universe,* quoted in Electric Universe video: *More Big Problems for Big Bang.*
70. ThunderboltsProject video: *More Big Problems for Big Bang.*
71. Video: Rupert Sheldrake – The Science Delusion Banned TED talk.
72. Dr Edi Bilimoria, *Aether – The Transcript,* p101.
73. Nature, 15/2/2001, *Initial Sequencing and Analysis of the Human Genome.*
74. Rupert Sheldrake, *The Science Delusion,* p168.
75. Rupert Sheldrake, *The Science Delusion,* p34-35.
76. Rudolf Steiner, An *Outline of Esoteric Science,* Anthroposophic Press, 1997.
77. John Horgan, *The End of Science – Facing the limits of Knowledge in the twilight of the Scientific Age.* 1997.
78. http://milesmathis.com/guth.pdf
79. Keith Francis, *Rudolf Steiner and The Atom,* Adonis Press, 2012, p188.
80. Rupert Sheldrake, Youtube video: *Rupert Sheldrake and Mark Vernon – Beyond Physicalism.*
81. https://www.the-scientist.com/?articles.view/articleNo/33719/title/Science-s-Reproducibility-Problem/
82. http://www.nature.com/news/1-500-scientists-lift-the-lid-on-reproducibility-1.19970
83. Mark Anderson, New Scientist, 18/3/2017, p28.
84. Stacy McGaugh, New Scientist, 18/3/2017, p33.
85. http://milesmathis.com/caven.html

86. Miles Mathis: *Another Hole in Celestial Mechanics.*
    http://milesmathis.com/cm2.html
87. Rudolf Steiner, *The Fourth Dimension,* Anthroposophic Press 2001,
    p128, from a lecture given on 15/10/1920.
88. Keith Francis, *Rudolf Steiner and the Atom,* p178.
89. Keith Francis, *Rudolf Steiner and the Atom,* p100.
90. Albert Einstein in a letter to Max Born, 1924. *Rudolf Steiner and the
    Atom,* p204.
91. Keith Francis, *Rudolf Steiner and the Atom,* p187.
92. Keith Francis, *Rudolf Steiner and the Atom,* p212.
93. https://en.wikipedia.org/wiki/Three-body_problem
94. Rudolf Steiner lecture of 19/9/1922, quoted on p 292 of
    *Awareness-Life-Form,* 2001
95. Rudolf Steiner lecture of 10/5/1924. *From Beetroot to Buddhism,*
    Rudolf Steiner   Press, p175. (Different translation)
96. Irmgard Rossmann, *The Etheric, Broadening Science through
    Anthroposophy,* Temple Lodge, 2017, p90.
97. Rudolf Steiner, 28/6/1908, *The Fourth Dimension,* Anthroposophic
    Press, 2001, p90.
98. Rudolf Steiner, 22/4/1909, *The Fourth Dimension,* Anthroposophic
    Press, 2001, p92.
99. Rudolf Steiner, 24/5/1905, *The Fourth Dimension,* Anthroposophic
    Press, 2001, p41.
100. Ernst Marti, *The Four Ethers,* p26. Available as pdf.
101. https://en.wikipedia.org/wiki/Rampart_crater
102. Rudolf Steiner, lecture 12/9/1924, *The Book of Revelation and the
    work of the priest,* Rudolf Steiner Press, 1998, p109.
103. Donald Tyson, *Three Books of Occult Philosophy,* Llewellyn
    Publications, p748.
104. Ernst Marti, *The Four Ethers,* p26.
105. John R R Searl, *The Law of the Squares,* books 1-17,
    searlsolution.com, segmagnetics.com.
106. Rudolf Steiner, *The Work of Secret Societies in the World,*
    23/12/1904. Keith Francis, *Rudolf Steiner and the Atom,* p47.
107. John R R Searl, *The Law of the Squares,* Book 1.

108. Robert Dickter, *Number Time Archetype, The Significance of Magic Squares in China and the West,* 2014. https://www.numbertimearchetype.com/

109. Rudolf Steiner, 15/10/1920, *The Fourth Dimension,* p129.

110. Rudolf Steiner, 12/4/1922, *The Fourth Dimension,* p150.

111. Nick Thomas, *Science Between Space and Counterspace,* Temple Lodge Publishing, 2008.

112. Rudolf Steiner, from *Goethes Naturwissenschaftliche Schriften,* Dornach, 1926. Quoted by Wachsmuth, *The Etheric Formative Forces in Earth, Cosmos and Man,* Anthroposophical Publishing Co, 1932, p23.

113. Guenther Wachsmuth, *The Etheric Formative Forces in Earth, Cosmos and Man,* Anthroposophical Publishing Co, 1932.

114. Guenther Wachsmuth, *The Etheric Formative Forces in Earth, Cosmos and Man,* Anthroposophical Publishing Co, 1932, p39-40.

115. Ernst Marti, *The Four Ethers* (pdf) and *The Etheric,* Temple Lodge, 2017.

116. Dion Fortune, *The Mystical Qabalah,* Fraternity Sanctum Regnum, 2008.

117. Dion Fortune, *The Mystical Qabalah,* Fraternity Sanctum Regnum, 2008, p45.

118. Patrice Chaplin, *The Portal,* Quest books, 2010, p127.

119. Dion Fortune, *The Mystical Qabalah,* Fraternity Sanctum Regnum, 2008, p37.

120. Aristotle, *On The Heavens,* quoted by Ernst Marti, *The Four Ethers,* p1.

121. Joseph P Farrell, *Reich of the Black Sun,* Adventures Unlimited Press, 2004 and Nicholas Goodrick-Clarke, *Black Sun,* New York University Press, 2002.

122. Walter Russell, *A New Concept of the Universe,* The University of Science and Philosophy, 1989

123. https://en.wikipedia.org/wiki/Sunita_Williams

124. http://cmex.ihmc.us/voviews/CRATERS.HTM

125. http://www.gillevin.com/Mars/Reprint125_files/Reprint125-SPIE-2003-Color-Paper.htm, http://www.goroadachi.com/etemenanki/mars-hiddencolors.htm
126. Andrew Johnson, *Secrets of the Solar System,* 2018, p153.
127. http://mars-news.de/color/blue.html
128. https://www.space.com/25577-mars-rover-opportunity-solar-panels-clean.html
129. Youtube video: *Former NASA Scientist claims conspiracy about Mars photo.*
130. http://www.openminds.tv/scientist-believes-evidence-alien-life-mars-destroyed/26012
131. Spirit Rover, Sol 386, Microscopic imager, https://mars.nasa.gov/mer/gallery/all/2/m/386/2M160631572EFFA2K1P2936M2M1.HTML
132. Opportunity Rover, Sol 3720, Microscopic imager, https://mars.nasa.gov/mer/gallery/all/1/m/3720/1M458433044EFFCEQKP2955M2M1.HTML
133. http://journalofquantumphysics.cosmology.com/ApotheciaOnMars.html and Youtube video: Mars: Alien Life Lawsuit: Rhawn Joseph Claims NASA is involved in a coverup over Mars.
134. Youtube videos: *Mars Microbes – Ron Bennett,* and *Life Found Moving on the Mars Phoenix Lander.*
135. https://www.space.com/14526-dead-mars-spacecraft-photos-spirit-phoenix.html
136. http://www.richplanet.net/starship_main.php?ref=192&part=1 , http://www.richplanet.net/starship_main.php?ref=193&part=1 , Or Youtube video: Richplanet TV: Evidence of NASA's Mars Rover Deception
137. Fred Seddon, *A Hypothesis: The Opportunity and Curiosity Mars Rovers are situated on Earth,* 2016, p58-64, Available from Richplanet.net/catalog/
138. Youtube video: Curiosity Rover Begins Mars Mission.
139. http://epsinantarctica.blogspot.co.uk/2008/12/what-are-we-doing-here.html

140. Curiosity Rover, Sol 52, Mastcam Right at 15:26:54 UTC, Mastcam Left at 15:27:52 UTC and Mastcam Left at 15:32:25 UTC. https://mars.nasa.gov/msl/multimedia/raw/?s=52&camera=MAST%5F

141. Curiosity Rover, Sol 77, Mastcam Right at 05:20:28 UTC. https://mars.nasa.gov/msl/multimedia/raw/?rawid=0077MR0005750010103776E01_DXXX&s=77

142. Third angle for triangulation: Curiosity Rover, Sol 55, Navcam Right at 18:43:25 UTC, Azimuth $314^0$, Elevation $-13^0$. http://curiosityrover.com/synth/?camera=NR&station=19

143. https://astroengineer.wordpress.com/2010/04/07/a-curiosity-of-spirit-full-document/

144. Richard D Hall, *A Hypothesis: The Opportunity and Curiosity Rovers are Situated on Earth.* 2016, p50. Available from Richplanet.Net.

145. Dr Judy Wood, *Where Did The Towers Go?* Published by The New Investigation, 2010.